TEACHING PRIMARY ENGLISH SERIES

SERIES EDITOR
JENI RILEY

Teaching Reading

at Key Stage 1
and Before

JENI RILEY

First published in 1999 by:
Stanley Thornes (Publishers) Ltd

Reprinted in 2004 by:
Nelson Thornes Ltd
Delta Place
27 Bath Road
CHELTENHAM
GL53 7TH
United Kingdom

05 06 07 08 / 11 10 9 8 7 6 5 4 3

A catalogue record for this book is available from the British Library

ISBN 0 7487 3516 X

Page make-up by The Florence Group, Stoodleigh, Devon

Printed and bound in Slovenia
by Delo tiskarna by arrangement with Korotan-Ljubljana

Contents

Dedication

For Roy, Nicky and Sacha, Benjamin and William

Acknowledgements

There are many people without whom this book would not exist.

Firstly, this series was conceived by Francis Dodds, formerly editor at Stanley Thornes, who thought of the idea and persuaded me to believe in it also. Neal Marriott took over as midwife to the series on Francis' departure. I am grateful to them both.

Secondly, I would like to thank Andrew Burrell for his work in tracking down research journal articles in the early stages of the writing.

Thirdly, I would like to thank busy people who have read drafts and offered their comments, Angela Hobsbaum and Rhona Stainthorp. I am indebted to Nicholas Bielby, the author of the companion volume *Teaching Reading at Key Stage 2* who has been hugely generous with both his time and his insight – his suggestions have improved the book. I especially valued Nicholas' keen and refreshing sense of humour.

The authors and publishers would also like to thank the MIT Press for permission to reproduce the figure on pages ix and 86.

Every effort has been made to contact copyright holders, and we apologise if any have been overlooked.

Jeni Riley
January 1999

The Teaching Primary English series

The importance of literacy for individuals and society cannot be overstated. This series of six complementary volumes supports the government's initiatives to raise standards in reading and writing. At the individual level, literacy determines personal growth, quality of life, self-image and the ability to function in the world. Being literate opens up opportunities, in an increasingly information-rich world, to access knowledge, to make choices and to achieve self-fulfilment. At national level, the smooth functioning and economic prosperity of a society depends upon a well-educated, flexible and highly skilled workforce.

> *Literacy is fundamental to thinking, to formal education, and to life-long learning. The link between high levels of literacy and academic success occurs, initially, through allowing individuals access to the curriculum, and secondly, through enabling them to achieve success educationally.*

(McGaw, Long, Morgan and Rosier, 1989)

THE NEED FOR HIGHER LEVELS OF LITERACY

Schools continually strive to maintain literacy standards, but with higher and higher levels of literacy required by modern society, more is demanded of them. Reading and writing have become even more crucial with the increased use of information and communications technology, although the production and form of texts are changing with the advent of fax, e-mail and the Internet. More has to be done to enable teachers to meet the greater demands placed upon them.

THE IMPORTANCE OF PRIMARY EDUCATION IN IMPROVING STANDARDS OF LITERACY

Primary schools and, in particular, the early years of education, are key to the success of any literacy drive. There is a body of research evidence that supports the claim that the foundations of literacy are laid in the first two years of school. I have argued elsewhere that a positive early start to school benefits pupils for the whole of their school careers (Riley, 1996). Furthermore, researchers in Australia suggest that efforts to correct literacy difficulties after the third grade (year) are largely unsuccessful:

> *Students who fail to make progress in literacy during the first two years of school rarely catch up with their peers and are at risk of becoming low achievers who are alienated with school and drop out at the earliest opportunity.*

(Kennedy, Birman and Demaline, 1986)

Conversely, there is empirical evidence that supports the view that it is possible for all children, except a very small percentage, to be successfully taught to read and write (Piluski, 1994). This encouraging evidence comes from the evaluations of the effectiveness of whole-school programmes such as *Success for All* (Slavin *et al.*, 1996) and an intervention programme, *Reading Recovery* (Hurry, 1995).

HOW ARE LITERACY STANDARDS TO BE RAISED?

It is clear from the American and Australian experience that class teachers cannot raise literacy standards alone and simply by working harder (Crevola and Hill, 1998). However, dramatic improvements can be achieved with comprehensive programmes that embrace 'system and school-wide commitment and co-ordination' (ibid.)

As Crevola and Hill (1998) suggest, the principles that underpin comprehensive initiatives to raise standards of literacy are that:

- there needs to be an attitude shift. High expectations and a belief that all children can be successful are the essential first step
- there is a need for a detailed, systematic and on-going record of progress to be kept on every pupil. This information guides decision-making regarding identification of, and intervention relating to, children 'at risk' and monitoring the teaching and learning of all
- good teaching needs to be targeted at raising standards of literacy. Such a requirement demands teachers who are well trained and who understand the literacy process; additional in-service opportunities are needed to support class teachers in their development of new modes of pedagogy and co-ordinating the programme across the school
- intervention programmes need to be available for the children who, despite effective teaching, fail to make progress
- strong links need to be in place between schools and their pupils' homes and communities.

Concern was identified by the Labour Party's Literacy Task Force in 1996, and the National Literacy Strategy, with the above characteristics, was planned and introduced in the United Kingdom in September 1998. As well as the introduction of this programme, initial teacher education received increasingly prescriptive directives on how the country's primary teachers should be trained (DfEE Circulars 10/97 and 4/98).

THE SERIES

The underlying principle

> . . .*that almost all children will become literate more easily and fully if they are given systematic help which is based on a good understanding of the nature of the enterprise but which never fails to respect them as individual learners.*

(Donaldson, 1993, p. 57)

This series of six complementary and interconnecting volumes re-affirms a wide and balanced ideological base for teaching language and literacy in primary schools and one that builds on existing successful provision. Such a view of the teaching and learning of English is informed by research evidence and established educational principles. The books aim to provide primary teacher educators, primary teachers and students with the knowledge, understanding and skills that are required to teach English effectively and imaginatively in primary classrooms. The intention is also to view reading in a wide frame of reference. The series dovetails reading with writing into literacy and sees them as integral with, and inseparable from, speaking and listening.

Previous influences on the teaching of English

Concern about literacy standards in primary schools has been the driving force for the government initiatives referred to earlier. The teaching of English has been the source of much debate, and the recipient of fruitful and abundant research. Important initiatives such as the National Curriculum, the National Writing Project, the National Oracy Project and the LINC (Language in the National Curriculum) Project have contributed to the advancement of thinking to its present position regarding the teaching and learning of speaking and listening, reading and writing. There is a great deal to be understood by primary teachers to enable them to teach English well; and the support of literacy particularly in the early years of school requires great skill and a rich knowledge base of the theory which informs understanding and underpins practice.

The DfEE Circulars and the National Literacy Strategy

This series readily acknowledges the need for DfEE Circulars 10/97 and 4/98 and the value of the introduction of the National Literacy Strategy. For the first time in history all teacher education institutions will be designing courses of initial teacher education that have the same starting points for English, mathematics and science. All students will be taught how to teach the core subjects of the National Curriculum from the same viewpoints with the same emphases and using the same content. No longer is there room for personal preferences, ideologies or flights of fancy. The National Literacy Strategy provides in considerable detail the content to be covered by teachers at different stages of primary education, stipulating when and how it is to be addressed. This unification and prescription of the English curriculum and how it is to be taught will have an immense effect on primary teachers and their professional functioning. Whilst some will mourn the loss of the greater autonomy of the past, many will find the framework and the structure supportive and enabling. Pupils remaining in the same school, or moving from school to school, will benefit from the consistency of approach, and the clearly thought-out progression of teaching.

The above introduction might seem to render unnecessary a series of books on the teaching and learning of language and literacy. The authors would like to argue exactly the reverse; we consider that these government initiatives require a series of volumes to expand on the documents, to explain them from a theoretical standpoint and to provide an academic rationale for the practice suggested. I have suggested elsewhere (Riley, 1996) that teachers have to be extraordinarily knowledgeable about the processes involved if they are to enable their pupils to become effective users of spoken and written language.

Teachers are not technicians, they are professionals making complex and finely tuned judgements that inform their teaching. Primary teachers cannot be given the equivalent of a painting-by-numbers kit and told to teach it. This is as unthinkable as a surgeon being given a step-by-step guide on how to conduct a heart operation. Both require a thorough and deep understanding of what is involved, the processes at work and sound direction regarding proven successful practice. These volumes aim to flesh out the theoretical references that underpin the thinking, to fill in the gaps in the explanations so that teachers are better able to implement the National Literacy Strategy with confidence and genuine understanding.

PSYCHOLOGICAL PROCESSES AT WORK WHEN READING

The view of literacy held by this series is one based firmly on the evidence of psychological research.

The starting point for these volumes is that literacy is an inter-related process and needs to be taught in a balanced way: that is a way that takes into account the different aspects of the processing. This perspective is the one adopted by the government initiatives. Teachers, we believe, in order to teach reading effectively, need to have an understanding of the processing which takes place in order for an individual to be able to read.

Any methods of teaching reading that aim to be comprehensive need to look for an explanation of the literacy process that accounts for its complexity. Figure I.1 demonstrates the inter-relatedness of the different processes involved.

Figure I.1
The inter-relatedness of the reading process

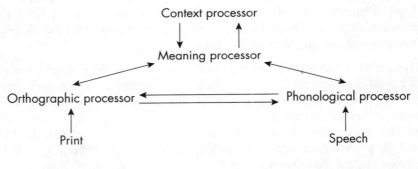

(Adams, 1990, p. 158)

This diagram shows how the two main strategies of reading work together to help the reader make sense of the text. The two strategies are the so-called 'top-down' processing and the 'bottom-up' processing of text.

Top-down processing skills

It can be seen from Figure I.1 that at the centre of the act of reading lies meaning-making, which fulfils the whole purpose of the activity. The context of the grammar and the meaning allows the reader to be supported in the task of decoding by being primed to expect what words might come next. The use of context is described as top-down processing and is in turn supported by the child's knowledge of the world, the story as a whole, the cover, the illustrations and the format of the book.

Bottom-up processing skills: sound awareness and print awareness

In order to read text, readers have to realise that there is a connection between the sounds that are spoken and the written marks on the page. Very crudely and simply this is the understanding that there is a written code (the alphabet) that represents the sounds of speech. There are various stages of progress as readers work towards this understanding.

On the way to learning to read, the child has to be able to hear and distinguish between the different words and then to discriminate between the constituent sounds in words (phonemic segmentation). These are then decoded from the letters and groups of letters on the printed page. The child who has this ability is said to understand grapheme–phoneme (letter–sound) correspondence. This aspect of reading is shown clearly in Figure I.1. An appreciation of the visual aspects of print (orthographic processing) and the identification of the aural sounds of spoken language (phonological processing) develops side by side, and the inter-relationship ensures that each complements the other. This processing is referred to as bottom-up or decoding skills.

Both top-down and bottom-up processing strategies have to be functioning if children are to learn to read successfully and speedily. Teachers need to know how to teach reading so that the whole processing system is developed and can operate effectively. This is the important principle that underpins the series and the two books on the teaching of reading in particular (*Teaching Reading at Key Stage 1 and Before* and *Teaching Reading at Key Stage 2*).

The authors of the volumes reaffirm their belief that:

> *Means must be found to ensure that all children's first experiences of reading and writing are purposeful and enjoyable. Only in this way will they be drawn into applying their meaning-making strategies to the task of making sense of written language. Only in this way will they learn to exploit the full symbolic potential of language and so become fully literate.*

(Wells, 1987, p. 162)

Jeni Riley, Series Editor
January 1999

References

Adams, M. J. (1990) *Beginning to Read: Thinking and Learning about Print*, MIT Press, Cambridge, Massachusetts

Crevola, C. A. and Hill, P. W. (1998) 'Evaluation of a whole-school approach to prevention and intervention in early literacy', *Journal of Education for Students Placed at Risk*, 3 (2), 133–57

DfEE (1997) Circular 10/97 and DfEE (1998) Circular 4/98, *Teaching: High Status, High Standards*, DfEE, London

Donaldson, M. (1989) 'Sense and sensibility: some thoughts on the teaching of literacy', Occasional Paper No. 3, Reading and Language Information Centre, University of Reading. Reprinted in R. Beard (ed.) (1993) *Teaching Literacy: Balancing Perspectives*, Hodder and Stoughton, London

Hurry, J. (1995) 'What is so special about Reading Recovery?' *Curriculum Journal*, 7 (1), 93–108

Kennedy, M. M., Birman, B. F. and Demaline, R. E. (1986) *The Effectiveness of Chapter 1 Services*, Office of Educational Research and Improvement, US Department of Education, Washington, DC

McGaw, B., Long, M. G., Morgan, G. and Rosier, M. J. (1989) *Literacy and Numeracy in Australian Schools*, ACER Research Monograph No. 34, ACER, Hawthorn, Victoria

Piluski, J. J. (1994) 'Preventing reading failure: a review of five effective programmes', *Reading Teacher*, 48, 31–9

Riley, J. L. (1996) *The Teaching of Reading: The Development of Literacy in the Early Years of School*, Paul Chapman Publishing, London

Slavin, R. E., Madden, N. A., Dolan, N. J., Wasik, B. J., Ross, S. M., Smith, L. J. and Dianda, M.(1996) 'Success for all: a summary of research', *Journal of Education for Students Placed at Risk*, 1, 41–76

Wells, C. G. (1987) *The Meaning Makers: Children Learning Language and Using Language to Learn*, Hodder and Stoughton, London

Learning to speak and learning to think 1

When you have read this chapter, you should:

- understand how children learn to talk and the stages of language development

- understand how adults can promote language development both at home and at school

- know how teachers can capitalise on the child's competence in spoken language to develop reading and writing.

Introduction

Language is the most powerful tool in the development of any human being. It is undeniably the greatest asset we possess. A good grasp of language is synonymous with a sound ability to think. In other words language and thought are inseparable.

(Vygotsky, 1986)

Children's ability to use language and to think is, in the first instance, a matter of oracy – their ability to speak and listen. Learning to read and write both depends upon their existing (oral) language skills *and* extends them. Literacy extends their language and thinking not only by opening up new sources of knowledge, but also by its nature. It does this in two ways.

- First, in speech, meaning is often implicit, depending on the speaker and listener sharing a situation. For example, in giving instructions, a speaker may say, 'Look, you do it like this'. The meaning is 'embedded' in the on-going situation. But instructions given in writing need to be much more explicit and organised. In its written form, language is 'disembedded' from the immediate situation, creating its own explicit, language-dependent, conceptual world (as when you are lost in a novel).
- Secondly, in its written form, language itself more readily becomes an object of perception in ways that develop reflectivity – it can be seen, reviewed and inspected.

LEARNING TO COMMUNICATE

There cannot be an adult who has worked with, or merely been in the company of, very young children who is not amazed at their capacity to communicate, and at their ability to do so without ambiguity. The young child astonishes us with her command and rapid acquisition of spoken language. The 10-month-old infant pointing to a beaker of juice or jar of biscuits with increasing tension in gesture and cry leaves an adult in no doubt as to the intended message. The young toddler holding up her arms and refusing to make any independent movement will ensure the lift to a car or into a buggy. In a short period of time, indeed after a passage of only a few months, the child is able to communicate desires and concerns through speech and action, followed later by speech alone.

Chomsky (1957) wrote that 'language is a window on the mind' and that through studying the way that children become users of spoken language we, as experienced language users, can gain an insight into the way that the minds of these young learners are working. We can observe the manner in which they organise sentences, how they over-generalise grammatical rules and then dismantle their own hypotheses in order to learn the correct forms. Not only are we offered a glimpse of the intellectual mechanism that is at work, but we also become aware of the preoccupations and interests of the child and her world as it impacts on her growing consciousness.

The stages of language development

Children are propelled into the ability to speak through the twin processes of their own drive to communicate and the desire of the care-giving adults to enable the child to occupy a full place in their world of shared meanings. Adults, it would appear, are motivated to talk to babies but, similarly, infants are programmed to respond with their own communicative skills and, according to Chomsky (op. cit.), they possess an innate ability to process the language around them.

Communication begins with the building of a relationship between the mother (most frequently) and the new-born infant from the first few days of life. This bonding stems from, and signifies, a mutual enjoyment of one another. The establishment of this relationship is manifested by babies as young as one week old preferring to gaze at a human face rather than other objects, however interesting, patterned or mobile (Trevarthan, 1975, cited in Harris, 1992). Researchers are in agreement that babies and their carers are able to engage in mutually satisfying and conversational-type activities by five or six weeks. This prototype of conversation is demonstrated by the variety of turn-taking actions such as mouth-opening, tongue-poking, eye gazing and vocalising, all of which occur, most commonly, at care-giving and changing times. These behaviours soon become ritualised. The activities are crucial as precursors to speech as they reinforce the supportive roles that speaker and listener need to adopt in order to maintain communication. Also, as Whitehead (1997) suggests, these activities are:

> *something to do with the complex business of getting two minds in contact, because the exchange of meanings and language is at the centre of human communication.*

(Whitehead, 1997, p. 4)

The interactive behaviours become more elaborate and prolonged, the smiling, cooing, chuckling and pointing develop into games of 'peek-a-boo', throwing and retrieving of objects, and hide, find and show. Playful actions and sounds, often repeated, maintain pleasurable response and prepare the way for a true conversation.

Early speech: the first word

The articulation of the first word is not a clear-cut event. The sounds made by the infant initially are playful and random and the baby's phonological production mechanism is immature. This makes word identification difficult. Whitehead suggests that for an utterance to be considered a 'word', it needs to fulfil the following criteria, that:

- *it is produced and used spontaneously by the child;*
- *it is identified by the caregiver who is the authority on what the child says (Nelson, 1973); and that*
- *it occurs more than once in the same context or activity (Harris, 1992).*

(cited by Whitehead, 1997, p. 5)

The first word is considered to be a developmental milestone and can be detected as early as 9 months old on occasions (Halliday, 1975), but more usually at around the first birthday. The initial utterance offers insight into the child and her personal situation. The name of a pet, a food, a drink, a comfort blanket or toy reflect the main preoccupations of these young minds, sometimes even before the time-honoured 'Mummm-aa' and 'Daddadaaa'. The richness of the meaning embedded in single-word utterances is described as a semantic field by linguists, and is specific both to context and to each individual child.

CASE STUDY

A personal vocabulary

My daughter at 15 months, when living on a military base, cried 'Dadaaa' to every blushing teenage cadet in uniform she saw as she was pushed in her pram. Her response to a male in military dress was habitual and of abiding fascination. Another 14-month-old child I know has the sole working vocabulary of 'I'm gorgeous!' and 'tractor'. The phrase he repeats parrot-fashion for the amusement of adults, but the noun denotes a current obsession. 'No' and (less usefully to the child!) 'Yes' are the first universal early words understood by the world that carry unambiguous meaning.

1 Learning to speak develops initially from the need to express a deeply personal concern or preoccupation. Can you think of examples of a child learning to talk and what her first words were?
2 Compare with a colleague and see if you can identify the main categories of the first words.

The two-word stage

The child experiments with speech as she approaches 2 years old, and in so doing she becomes more inventive and adventurous in her use of language. Combinations of words are attempted and if they obtain the intended results, the structures are used again and again and perfected. The two-word stage relies on intonation to achieve full linguistic clarity. For example, 'Daddy house' can mean 'This is Daddy's house' or said with a rising intonation might mean 'Is Daddy in the house?'

CASE STUDY

Communicating desires

My grandson, Benjamin, at 19 months pronounced 'Choclat! fetch it! – shall us?' The first three words exercised firm, clear expectation and then the softer, wheedling 'shall us?' applied persuasive pressure. The ability to exert authority is not curtailed by a limited command of speech structures. At this age, determination and a shrewd judgement of people wins over linguistic expertise.

A few months later, after an afternoon of vigorous activity when I am baby-sitting, Benjamin, now about 2 years old, spied his father's forbidden juggling balls on a

continued...

high shelf. 'I juggle now,' he stated with firm resolve. With a clear demonstration of premature senility, I reached for the box of balls. The ensuing damage caused by balls being enthusiastically hurled into the air succeeded in getting us both into a good deal of trouble!

This stage of language development, involving the combination of two or three words, is informed by an application of the rules of grammar. The ability to combine words in this way to express meaning denotes an appreciation of syntactical structure that has intrigued and excited linguists for years. The rules that children generate for themselves may not be conventional, nor are they those that they have heard used by an adult previously, but there is an applied logic and a system, and the end result is, indisputably, functional.

DEVELOPING SPEECH

Through the pre-school years the child is exposed to many language-enriching experiences. Her spoken language is developed through being surrounded by conversation, through the multiple interactions she has with different people, through watching and listening to television, through chanting rhymes and poetry. Alongside this, the child experiences the speech-enhancing effect of written language. She is exposed to and encouraged to interact with books, through hearing stories, looking at and talking about the illustrations, enjoying magazines, receiving cards, and seeing notes, lists and letters written and having them read to her.

By the age of 4, most children have acquired at least 1,600 words and can understand many more (Crystal, 1987). The physiological mechanisms to produce speech are now well-developed and enunciation is more intelligible and clearer. The powerful intellectual capacity to exploit the rules of language that the child has worked out for herself, not merely to repeat language, is demonstrated by her over-generalisation of past tenses as in 'goed' and 'see-ed', the logical regularisation of plurals with 'mouses' and 'foots', and the transformation of nouns into verbs, such as 'boxing' an object. These inventions remind us that language acquisition is not simply imitation. The child constructs language in order to communicate, to get things done, to learn and to comment on the world and, in short, to make meaning.

Influences beyond home

Once at school, the child becomes involved with a wider social community which requires her to communicate and function with many different people for a variety of purposes. Literacy now has greater and greater impact on spoken language development. Speech structures become more complex and literary influences are evident in the child's oral language patterns and vocabulary. The presence of more elaborate connectives becomes evident, as does the awareness of cause and effect when the child experiments with constructions such as 'What I think is. . .', followed by 'because. . .' and 'When I get round to it I will. . .'. Ambivalence and uncertainty are expressed with 'maybe', 'perhaps' and 'probably', and the passive voice is understood but probably not used. Vocabulary expands with the acquisition of technical and subject-specific words needed to meet the linguistic demands of school-based learning, as the pupil now has the opportunity to experience specialist areas of the curriculum.

CLASSIFICATIONS OF LANGUAGE FUNCTIONS

The development of spoken language, we have seen, is dependent upon the opportunity and the need to communicate. Gradually, the use of language broadens through greater linguistic expertise and advancing conceptual and social maturity. Halliday developed a classification system for the different functions of language. The following shows well, using only three examples from his system, how children use language in increasingly complex ways. First, children see the need to employ an instrumental function of language, that is the use of speech in order 'to get things done' (Halliday, 1975). Later, the functions become refined into both regulatory, or controlling of the behaviour of others, and the interactional, which is concerned with the establishment and then the maintenance of relationships with others. This reflects the growing complexity of the individual's social interactions through childhood. Primary teachers need to be aware of the different dimensions of function and use of oral language to be able to determine the level of a child's growing control.

Wilkinson (1982) suggests another classification of language which compares interestingly to that of Halliday. This is based on questions surrounding three basic activities 'Who am I?', 'Who are you?' and 'Who or what is it, was it, will be?'

> *Who am I?*
> 1 *Establishing and maintaining self*
> 2 *Language for analysing self*
> 3 *Language for expressing self (for celebrating or despairing)*

Who are you?
   4 *Establishing and maintaining relationships*
   5 *Co-operating*
   6 *Empathising, understanding the other*
   7 *Role playing, mimicry*
   8 *Guiding, directing the other*

Who/what is he/she/it?
   9 *Giving information*
   10 *Recalling past events*
   11 *Describing past events (present)*
   12 *Predicting future events: statement of intention, statement of hypothesis, what might happen*
   13 *Analysing, classifying*
   14 *Explaining, giving reasons for*
   15 *Exploring asking questions, etc.*
   16 *Reflecting on own/others' thoughts and feelings.*

(Wilkinson, 1982, p. 56)

Children gradually learn to express their needs, thoughts and feelings more precisely and articulately, and in turn, so their ideas develop with the ability to talk. Using language more precisely enables pupils to generalise, to categorise, to manipulate ideas and to explore notions of cause and effect. Opportunities to use spoken language in a variety of ways and for many different purposes need to be offered in reception and Year 1 classes so that pupils fully develop their ability not only to use language effectively but also to use it to think.

SUPPORTING PRE-SCHOOL LANGUAGE DEVELOPMENT

The first section of this chapter has briefly charted the young child's acquisition of speech from early infancy through to the end of Key Stage 1. Now we will consider what factors in the home environment encourage the development of spoken language and what appears to be less supportive. The Bristol Study (Wells, 1987) provides research evidence into this aspect of child development. The research project studied the language development of 128 children from the age of 13 months through to starting mainstream school. This project offers a rich source of information on the differing domestic situations, the material circumstances and the variety and type of adult support of the children involved, and compared it with differing levels of emerging linguistic competence. Wells and his colleagues provide informed speculation on the relationship between the progress of the children and their circumstances and their experiences.

The research team found great variation in the rate at which children acquire spoken language. They attempted to determine the reasons for this. Adults, it would appear, are intuitively very good at enabling infants to crack the code of speech. Parents imbue their babies' pre-vocalisations with meaning; they support interaction with sustained eye-gaze, encouragement and evident enjoyment. Mothers speak to their children in a manner described by psychologists as 'motherese' which is highly facilitative to language development. It is a form of speech that is raised in pitch and is simple and repetitive. The child's utterance is frequently expanded upon for the purpose of clarification and this also provides intuitive tutoring. If the child says, for example, 'Dan sock!', the adult is likely to respond 'Yes, that *is* Dan's sock. He must have his red socks on this morning.'

All the evidence is that children learn language best not through drills and instruction, but when adults attend to, and are interested in, what children say and mean, and engage them in real conversation. Children's language skills need personal interaction in order to develop. If one believes that a child learns through being taught to speak rather as one would teach a parrot, it has important implications for the way in which the adults closest to that child should interact with her. Wells is clear from the evidence of his study that this is not the case. In fact, he cites examples where it is plainly counter-productive and discouraging when a mother deliberately sets out to teach her child, as in the following case study.

CASE STUDY

Supporting language development?

'Thomas (age 25 months) has seen a plate of biscuits (cookies) on the table. His first utterance consists of three words, but only the third is intelligible.

Thomas:	* * biscuits.
Mother:	Those were got specially 'cos we had visitors at the weekend. Who came to see Tommy? Who came in a car?
Thomas:	See Grannie Irene uh car.
Mother:	Grannie Irene's coming next weekend. But who came last weekend?
Thomas:	Auntie Gail <u>in a train</u>.
Mother:	<u>Auntie Gail</u>'s coming. They're coming on the train, yes.
Thomas:	Colin uh Anne <u>a train.</u>

continued...

Mother:	Colin – Colin and Anne came in the car, didn't they?
Thomas:	Colin uh Anne. Colin uh Anne.
Mother:	Yes.
Thomas:	Colin uh Anne. Colin uh Anne.
Mother:	Colin and Anne came in the train.
Thomas:	In uh train. Auntie train.
Mother:	No, not Auntie train, darling. Auntie Gail and Grannie are coming on the train on Friday.
Thomas:	Auntie Gail in uh train.
Mother:	That's right.'

(Wells, 1987, p. 49)

1 What effect do you think this kind of 'teaching' language has on Thomas?
2 What is he really interested in?

What, then, does appear to be valuable? If we take the stance that children are largely constructors of their own personal version of spoken language, perhaps it can be argued that adults have little to contribute to the process? This is patently not true. In order to progress, the child needs feedback on the effectiveness of her linguistic efforts, to talk to people and, through conversational exchange, to test hypotheses about the way that language works and to have the hypotheses confirmed. The extent to which children have this opportunity is important. Wells identified a clear and positive relationship between those children who were exposed to a large number of conversations and the rate at which they developed. So, the amount of experience of talk is important but it is even more complex than that. Wells says:

> What seems to be important is that, to be most helpful, the child's experience of conversation should be in a one-to-one situation in which the adult is talking about matters that are of interest and concern to the child, such as what he or she is doing, has done or plans to do, or about activities in which the child and adult engage together.

(Wells, 1987, p. 44).

The value of the shared experience is that it maximises the possibility of the meaning being appropriately interpreted by both participants and built upon further. The child, the less experienced language user, is supported through interest and the context and in this way is motivated into sustaining the dialogue. The role of the more experienced speaker, the adult, is crucial. Wells continues:

> *This therefore places a very great responsibility on the adult to compensate for the child's limitations and to behave in ways that make it as easy as possible for the child to play his or her part as effectively as possible.*

(Wells, 1987, p. 45)

Parents or carers are best placed to do this at this stage of spoken language development, as they have insight into the child's model of the world and her linguistic resources. This enables them to be skilful and co-operative listeners and to make a rich interpretation of the child's utterances. An example of a parent doing exactly that is given in the following case study.

CASE STUDY

Supporting language development

'In the first extract from the recordings of Mark, we see very clear examples of these strategies for sustaining and extending Mark's meanings:

Mark: [looking out of the window at the birds in the garden] Look at that. Birds Mummy.

Mother: Mm.

Mark: Jubs [birds].

Mother: [inviting Mark to extend his own meaning] What are they doing?

Mark: Jubs bread [Birds eating bread]

Mother [extending Mark's meaning] Oh, look! They're eating the berries, aren't they?

Mark: Yeh.

Mother: [extending and paraphrasing] That's their food. They have berries for dinner.

Mark: Oh.'

(Wells, 1987, p. 47)

1 Compare with the previous example of Thomas and his mother. What are the most obvious differences?
2 Why does Wells consider that this conversational experience is so valuable for a child?

The mother is adjusting her speech to take into account Mark's ability and is responding to him. The topic of conversation is one in which Mark is interested as he initiated it. The adult provides information on the topic and extends his understanding of the world. Mark is acting as a full participant with acknowledgments of his mother's contributions. As Wells says, it is a collaborative enterprise in which they both are engaged. Adults do not need to be over-analytical concerning the linguistic complexity of how exactly they are operating, but they do need to know that the value lies in the *way* they respond.

> *All that is required is that they be responsive to the cues that children provide as to what they are able to understand. Rather than adults teaching children, therefore, it is children who teach adults how to talk in such a way as to make it easy for them to learn.*

> (Wells, 1987, p. 48)

Children therefore play the major role in constructing their knowledge of oral language, although they are greatly facilitated in this by adults. Children who made less progress were not as frequently involved in one-to-one conversations or with adults who worked hard at trying to make mutual sense of a situation.

Conclusions of the Bristol Study

The teaching points that emerge for teachers, parents and carers from the findings of the Bristol study are as follows.

> *When the child appears to be trying to communicate, assume he or she has something important to say and treat the attempt accordingly.*

> *Because the child's utterances are often unclear or ambiguous, be sure you have understood the intended meaning before responding.*

> *When you reply, take the child's meaning as the basis of what you say next – confirming the intention and extending the topic or inviting the child to do so for him or herself.*

> *Select and phrase your contributions so that they are at or just beyond the child's ability to comprehend.*

> (Wells, 1987, p. 50)

SUPPORTING LANGUAGE DEVELOPMENT AT SCHOOL

We need now to look at the types of talk found in schools that are the most valuable for developing language. The research evidence demonstrates considerable variation between the home and the school setting. At home, children are very much more likely to initiate a conversation (in some of Wells' analyses the percentage is as high as 70 per cent) than at school. He cites several depressing incidences in which the teacher and the child appear to be talking completely at cross-purposes, with the result that both participants became frustrated and disinclined to repeat the experience. Mutual enjoyment is far from the experience of either participant. Little learning is likely to have occurred. Worse still, in the most striking of the examples cited (see the following case study), the impression that Rosie has given to her reception teacher is one of linguistic incompetence and this contrasts poorly with the transcripts taped at her home.

CASE STUDY

Supporting language development in the classroom?

'Child: Miss, I done it.
Teacher: [to Rosie] Will you put it on top?
Child: Miss, I done it, look.
[Several seconds pause]
Teacher: [to Rosie, pointing with finger at card] What are those things?
Child: Miss, I done it.
            Miss, I done it.
[Rosie drops something and then picks it up]
Teacher: [to Rosie] What are those things?
Child: Miss, <u>I done it</u>.
Teacher: [referring to skis in the picture] <u>Do you know</u> what they are called?
[Rosie shakes her head]
            What d'you think he uses them for? [Rosie looks at the card. The teacher turns to the other child's calendar] . . .
Teacher: [to Rosie, pointing at the skis on the card] What's – what are those?
[Rosie looks blank]
            What do think he uses them for?
Rosie: [rubbing one eye with the back of her hand] Go down.'

(Wells, 1987, p. 97)

1 Why do you think this conversational exchange is so unhelpful to Rosie?
2 What in your view might have made it more fruitful?

Barriers to effective language use and development

The obvious and inescapable issue in school is the unrealistic expectation that one teacher can communicate effectively with 30 or more small children. But this is not the only factor that militates against a supportive linguistic learning environment in the nursery, reception and Key Stage 1 classroom.

It is a fact of life that teachers have parental pressures and different agendas with which to cope; they have a prescribed curriculum to cover with National Curriculum Tasks and Tests, and the league tables are never far from their professional consciousness. This situation ensures that the interactions that occur in classrooms usually have a predetermined goal, an idea or concept to be encountered or a skill to be acquired. This situation is, in Wells' opinion, counterproductive to any kind of valuable learning and leads to the 'Guess what is in my mind?' phenomenon.

CASE STUDY

Supporting language development in the classroom?

'The third extract once again comes from a session involving the whole class, following the reading of *Elmer the Elephant*. In the course of a discussion of some of the pictures, Stella volunteers a personal anecdote:

Teacher:	Can you see what that elephant's got on the end of his trunk?
Children:	(laugh)
Teacher:	What is it?
Children:	A blower?
Teacher:	A blower – a party blower. It is funny isn't it?
Stella:	My-my-my brother brought one home from a party.
Teacher:	Did he? What does it do as well as blowing?
Stella:	Um.
First child:	(inaudible)
Teacher:	Sh! (signals she wants Stella to answer) What does it do?
Stella:	Mm! – the thing rolls out (makes an appropriate gesture).
Teacher:	Yes, the thing rolls down and rolls up again, doesn't it? But what does it do as well as unrolling and rolling up?
Stella:	Um.
Teacher:	Does it do anything else?
First child:	Squeaks.
Teacher:	Sh! (signals for Stella to answer) Does Adrian's squeak? – Adrian's blower squeak?
Stella:	(nods)
Teacher:	Does it?

continued...

> They usually squeak and they often have a little feather on it too, don't they? (intonation of finality)
> Children: Yes (chanted)
> Teacher: Well I think that's a lovely story.
> It's one of my favourites.'
>
> (Wells, 1987, p. 139)
>
> What might have made the point the teacher was trying to make clearer? If the teacher had a party blower to show the children would it have helped this discussion?

closed question
question to which there is only one right answer; tends to ask for information retrieval

open question
question to which there is more than one answer, or one way of answering; seeks information and at best prompts new thinking

This extract could be analysed productively and usefully on the type of questions most in evidence – child-initiated questions, teacher-initiated questions, and **open** and **closed questions.** The children ask no questions at all and the teacher appears to use only one category, namely, closed questions. The most important point to make from this fairly typical example of group discussion from the Bristol Study is that although several answers may well have been accurate in terms of logic, frequently only one answer is acceptable to the teacher. Young children can be observed desperately searching for clues from the adult's facial expression and body language, that might lead to the 'correct' response, before venturing a reply. Some will rarely volunteer a suggestion so impotised are they by this school 'game'. Wells makes a plea for teachers to adopt a flexible approach in their interactions with children so that if one of several answers is appropriate, alternative suggestions are accepted and developed. Doing this allows pupils to continue to offer responses and to participate in the collaborative act of meaning-making that is the nature of genuine conversational exchange.

Implications for practice

Spoken language will only flourish in an intellectually stimulating, activity-based, learning environment. Conversation develops from the necessity to talk 'to get things done', to question, to establish issues of importance, to find out about things of interest. The language-rich classroom will be a centre of experience and challenge from which purposeful discussion will follow. Talk cannot be manufactured artificially; it arises from curiosity and intrigue, and is highly specific and context-embedded. Becoming a fluent speaker depends on social interaction and this knowledge should influence the opportunities extended to children within the classroom environment. The adults that the child interacts with have great potential to enable her to talk differently and to experiment with using language that is different from the language she uses when talking to her peers. Teachers can probe and prompt pupils to learn to use language to convey meaning precisely as they learn, for example 'Why do you think the worm moves like that?', 'How would you describe the movement?'

Teachers of young children will be concerned with the way that activities are presented to their classes to ensure they offer a variety of learning approaches to appeal to several types of cognitive style. Children will be encouraged to contribute and function effectively in class discussion if treated courteously and appropriately with 'Thank you, Geraldine, that is a helpful suggestion, we could make our book like that. . .', etc., and in the way that the facilitative parent or carer intuitively supports the pre-school child.

WHAT CONTRIBUTES TO THE LITERACY PROCESS?

Spoken language

Learning to read and write is parasitic upon learning to speak. This is demonstrated by the relationship between learning to read and then understanding the way in which symbols represent speech. In addition, through the experience of literacy, the child gains an explicit knowledge to add to her considerable implicit knowledge about language. This explicit knowledge about language is expressed as 'language about language' (called **meta-language**, Clark, 1976) and includes the use of terms like 'word', 'sentence', 'phrase' and, with respect to writing, 'letter', 'capital letter' and 'full stop'.

meta-language
the technical term used to describe the properties of language; terms like 'sentence', 'word' and 'morpheme' are meta-linguistic terms

This linguistic awareness is at a surface level and at a deep structure level (grammatical features). Through spoken language acquisition and the focus on meaning, structure is learnt. An awareness of the structure of language is acquired as reading and writing are learned. An understanding, also, of the sound system and how it is represented by letters and groups of letters has to be achieved. This aspect of literacy learning is considered in depth in Chapters 2 and 3. As Adams (1990) says:

> For purposes of learning to read and write, . . . sub-units [of language] must be dug out of their normal, sub-attentional status. Children must push their attention down from the level of comprehension at which it normally works. Not surprisingly, the deeper into the system they push the harder it is to do. Thus awareness of clauses or prepositions develops earlier and more easily than awareness of words. Awareness of words develops earlier and more easily than the awareness of syllables. An awareness of syllables develops earlier and more easily than the awareness of phonemes.
>
> (Adams, 1990, pp 294–5)

As a result of attending school, the child's language develops and she learns to broaden her use of spoken language to accommodate new registers and functions with differing individuals in a variety of situations (Clay, 1991). Meanings become more precise and richer, vocabulary widens and sentence patterns become more complex. The child also becomes aware of constructions and literary conventions present in written language. She learns to use complex structures peculiar to narrative, such as 'As I walked down the road, I noticed. . .'.

Donaldson (1989) and Reid (1993) suggest the ways that the teaching of reading skills in the early years of schooling can capitalise on the learning that has occurred in the acquisition of speech. Reid describes these as bridges or links that can be established. They are:

- shared reading
- helping children to produce written language
- use of print embedded in the environment.

Shared reading

This approach has been formalised into one of the key methods for teaching reading in the National Literacy Strategy and is discussed in greater detail in Chapter 2. The potential value of an adult and child sharing books emanates from the research findings in the emergent literacy phase. The adult first provides the child with a **scaffold** of understanding through discussing the illustrations and the story, which enables the child to predict the situation and events of the story as a whole – the **global context** or 'big picture'. Three elements contribute to the context here. Two of the elements are local to the sentence: there is the developing meaning and there is the developing grammar of the sentence. This is called **local context.** Thirdly, there is the wider context of the whole story – everything that the child knows about life and about the structure, conventions and language of narrative.

The adult supports the child further by making the conventions of print explicit and providing the opportunity to become familiar with book language. Adults share books in this way at home, and increasingly opportunities exist for books to be shared in school. These opportunities should be capitalised upon as frequently as possible. The use of enlarged texts enables teachers to do this with small and larger groups of children.

Helping children to produce written language

Adults can support children to be part of the writing process by helping them with the encoding of speech, by writing for the children and making books with them. The use of commercially-

scaffold
a metaphor to indicate the external support or cognitive help an adult can give children while they are internally constructing or developing schemas or concepts

global context
the 'big picture' – the wider context of the whole story

local context
the elements that are local to the sentence – the developing meaning and the developing grammar of the sentence

produced materials to facilitate writing, such as *Breakthrough to Literacy* (Mackay *et al.*, 1970), can also be of great value. Pre-written words that can be selected and formed into sentences short-circuit the grapho-motor abilities of the very young child to make easier the link from thought to speech to print. Important understandings regarding the nature of a word as a unit of meaning and a letter as a representation of sound can be reinforced.

Use of print embedded in the environment

Children in the **logographic phase** of print processing (see Chapter 3, page 52) are able to recognise 'MacDonalds' and 'Weetabix' logos in context, through operating in a print-filled environment. At this stage, which begins before school, children learn to recognise familiar words as wholes, or **logograms**, without any notion of the alphabetic nature of their composition.

Reid suggests that teaching in schools should take greater advantage of this developing skill and use print in an embedded form to the maximum benefit, in the way that has been so valuable for the child in her pre-school encounters with print. Use can be made of labels on packaging, notices in public places and wall displays in school for learning to read.

logographic phase
the earliest phase of the sight-recognition of words

logogram
written symbol that represents a whole word, as in Chinese, or as with the ampersand (&)

THE LEARNING ENVIRONMENT

An enabling learning environment for literacy is one that also promotes the development of oracy. As discussed, in the years before school, almost all children have acquired a competence in language with a wide vocabulary and have learned how to employ a complex system of grammar. More importantly, the child has engaged in the problem-solving, intellectual task of shaping language to express her own thinking. Spoken language has enabled the child to structure experience, to make sense and to communicate.

Purposeful talk needs to underpin all language activities in the classroom. Written language now increasingly supports intellectual development and extends understanding of the world and people. Therefore, it is essential that the teacher views oracy and literacy as inter-related. The nursery and classroom have the potential to offer rich experience, activity and stimulation that promote the talk and discussion from which reading and writing will arise.

Play has been the vehicle through which much enabling language practice has occurred before school and can continue to be valuable in school. There are many different types of play. The following case study describes a child engaged in solitary play through which he rehearses his own life experience, his own story.

CASE STUDY

Storying

'The child talks to his toys about past events and goes over what has happened in different ways of explaining and telling:

"This is my mummy house, my daddy house,
my Billy house, my granny house,
Houses, houses, houses, his houses,
and mummy goes to work and Billy. . ."

For all that seems inconsequential, this early talk is by no means random. It performs many functions in children's language learning, but its relevance here is that it is story-telling, the beginning of knowing how to narrate.'

(Meek, 1982, p. 33)

1 What might a teacher want to discuss with the child if she observed such 'storying' occurring?
2 Think of the occasions when you have observed children narrate in this way.
3 What play materials are particularly valuable to promote this kind of language work?

The early years teacher will harness the pupil's predilection to play, to talk, to story and to make-believe by providing tempting opportunities to engage in such activities in the classroom. The home corner can be converted into a castle, a hospital, a post office, a Chinese restaurant, a travel agent, a book shop, or whatever else might stimulate activity, fantasy, language and literacy. This provision allows children to use talk to enhance their play and, in the process, talk is practised, experimented with and developed. Frequently, children will want to use writing and print in their play also.

The benefits of a well-organised classroom are obvious, but the benefits to literacy learning perhaps need to be made explicit. Language is greatly enhanced, as indeed is all learning, by a classroom with an organisational system that develops the autonomy of the children. This principle refers to both the physical organisation of furniture, materials and resources and also to the way that the learning of the children is managed, for example by providing opportunities for pupils to choose activities, and to justify their choices. Two obvious benefits occur from a considered, well-organised and managed classroom. The pupils' growth in confidence and self-reliance is a valuable attribute when learning to read and write. This self-reliance also provides the teacher with the time and opportunity to talk with children, to observe literacy behaviours and to cater for individual differences.

A rich learning environment provides opportunities for children to express their ideas in a variety of ways. Successful classrooms will share most of the following characteristics (adapted from Riley, 1996):

- an attractive environment, with play areas designed with the development of spoken and written language in mind
- the furniture arranged to facilitate many organisational situations and with storage for materials that are clearly labelled
- a well-maintained and well-equipped book area with a supply of high-quality fiction and poetry (and possibly non-fiction if this is not stored centrally in the school library)
- a plentiful supply of reading books of wide ranging interest and quality. These should provide structure and progression in sufficiently small steps to support all levels of reading ability. Storage needs to be logical (i.e. stored by level of difficulty), clear and accessible. Multiple copies of key books are essential for group reading and enlarged texts are crucial at nursery and reception levels
- an attractive, inviting book corner
- a well-supplied writing area where children can express thoughts, feelings and ideas
- all labels and notices at the appropriate height for the children, demonstrating a high standard of printing in order to provide a good model of typeface
- a variety of class-made books which are easily accessible
- audio-visual equipment that is accessible and that the children are able to use, for example language masters, audio-cassette recorders
- computers with concept keyboards and other appropriate software for literacy development
- reading support materials (including a variety of puzzles and games that encourage word play and specific focus on print) stored in an ordered way and accessible to the pupils
- a range of dictionaries, thesauruses and directories
- wall displays and charts that promote reading and discussion placed where children can see them, including alphabet friezes
- a listening area with stories available on tape, plus puppet theatre and story boards for mini-dramatisation (especially important for pupils for whom English is an additional language)
- word banks of topic and high-frequency keywords – see National Literacy Strategy *Framework for Teaching* (DfEE, 1998).

THE LANGUAGE EXPERIENCE APPROACH

This is the time-honoured approach adopted by most early years teachers. It capitalises on the natural interests and activities of the children in order to record their experiences and spoken language by writing and drawing for themselves and others. Adults using this approach are able to demonstrate the word-by-word conversion of speech into written language as the child dictates. The mechanism is a powerful one. The process is as follows.

1 The child is given an opportunity to have an. . .*experience*.
2 The adult encourages discussion and translates the thought into . . .*spoken language*.
3 The adult writes the transcription of the talk. . .*encoded into written language*.
4 The adult reads the text back to child. . .*decoded by reading*.
5 The child re-reads the text. . .*re-reading*.

The power of the literacy learning in the Language Experience Approach derives from the interest the child has in the content and the written language that is generated by her and for her. An additional benefit for learning is that the written language is in the natural speech patterns of the child. The Language Experience Approach uses both the encoding and the decoding processes jointly to effect learning, as each complements and reinforces the other.

All the day-to-day class happenings can be recorded and used as the talking, reading and writing focus of the day, whether it is the class topic or project, a visit to a place of interest, a visitor to the class, a science experiment, biscuits baked, a new baby – the possiblities are endless.

The text can reflect the thoughts of the children or others, the recounting of a happening in the genre of journalism or the retelling of a favourite story using the appropriate literary language of narrative.

The resulting product could take the form of a letter, a note, a beautifully crafted hand-made book, or a large wall story to accompany a picture or model.

The teacher's role in the Language Experience Approach

The teacher needs to be aware of the child as a learner, and to extend and to support both her spoken and written language. She also needs to make explicit the links between reading and writing in order to effect the bridge that is so valuable for literacy development (Reid, 1993). For this reason, the Language Experience

Approach has been embraced enthusiastically by early years teachers because it encompasses the support and reinforcement for all the inter-related aspects of the literacy process (see the series introduction, page vi). With this approach to the teaching of reading and writing, the decoding of the child's own words makes the literacy act especially meaningful and memorable, particularly in the earliest stages of reading. Prediction (i.e. the ability to read a word through using global and local context) is made easier because the text has been initially generated by the child and so comprehension is unlikely to present difficulties. Working with children as they generate text enables explicit demonstration of sound–symbol relationships, letter-by-letter as the words are encoded. The quality of the child's language is determined by the stimulus of the experience and the way in which it is discussed and developed into learning activities. This way of working with children mimics the parent at home by asking open questions, encouraging the child to reflect and comment further, to hypothesise and, most importantly, to share enjoyment and wonder. It begins with the child and what she is interested in and extends her understanding. As Clay says:

> When we try to provide experiences. . .we must go beyond the usual bounds of spontaneous learning in a free play situation or group learning from one teacher. The child's spontaneous wish to communicate about something which interests him at one particular moment should have priority and he must have adults who will talk with him, in simple, varied and grammatical language. We should arrange for language producing activities where adult and child must communicate to co-operate.

(Clay, 1979, pp 53–4)

It follows then for the teacher to work with that spoken communication and transform the child's words into the permanent record of a text.

Summary

We have discussed the acquisition of spoken language and the way that this is achieved through the child striving to communicate and to make meaning. The development of speech is promoted most effectively by interested adults who 'tune in' to the child's early attempts to talk by encouraging and expanding her language structures. This process is mirrored in school, despite the obvious drawback of one adult and many children, offering meaningful opportunities to the child to communicate orally and in writing.

The key points this chapter has addressed are:

● the stages of language development

● the way that adults support children as they learn to talk

● how oracy can be promoted in the classroom.

Further reading

Wells, C.G. (1987) *The Meaning Makers: Children Learning Language and Using Language to Learn*, London: Hodder & Stoughton
A very readable book describing the Bristol research study – an important text for all early years teachers to read.

Whitehead, M. (1997) *The Development of Language and Literacy*, London: Hodder & Stoughton
This is an accessible and interesting book on the development of spoken and written language, written by an experienced early years practitioner.

The links between oracy and literacy 2

When you have read this chapter, you should be able to:

- recognise the way that learning to read and write is parasitic on learning to speak

- be aware of the fundamental understanding that the child has to grasp about written language, i.e. that print is a permanent, unchanging representation of spoken language

- know what is meant by sampling, prediction, confirming and self-correcting strategies in the task of reading

- understand the role of the teacher in promoting progress.

Introduction

Reading is:

> *a message-gaining, problem-solving activity, which increases in power and flexibility the more it is practised.*

(Clay, 1979)

In the series introduction (page vi), an ideological stance is adopted regarding a model (or theoretical explanation) of the literacy process. There I argue that the literacy process is multi-faceted, interactive and inter-related. This makes it problematic when trying to decide the sequence in which the different aspects of the literacy process should be addressed. Inevitably, a hierarchy of importance is implied by a specific order in which topics are presented in a book. This is misleading in this instance and I would wish to suggest that the order here denotes a *developmental sequence*. Therefore, it would seem logical to follow a chapter on the acquisition of spoken language with a discussion of those features in the development of written language that can be viewed as having something in common with learning to talk.

THE CONNECTION BETWEEN LEARNING TO SPEAK AND LEARNING TO READ AND WRITE

In Chapter 1 it is suggested that learning to speak is achieved through learning how to make meaning. In many important and similar ways the child learns that written language also can fulfil the personal purpose of communication, for enjoyment and the acquisition of information. This crucial discovery, made 'through living in a print-filled world' (Goodman, 1980), is that written language makes sense and that this understanding is acquired through listening and watching experienced writers and readers and through becoming aware in a general sense of the meaning-fulness of logos and signs in the environment.

However, other writers provide different perspectives on the meaning-making processes at work in the early stages of getting to grips with symbolic representation. The child engages with the challenge of representing the world to herself and to others from many different and complex starting points.

OPERATING WITH SYMBOLS TO MAKE MEANING

Reading can be defined strictly as the process of taking meaning from print by identifying the written words in sequence. This process has two aspects – identifying the words, and understanding the meaning. The term 'reading' can also be usefully used with a wider ranging, metaphorical connotation, where the emphasis falls upon interpretation rather than on decoding, as in expressions like 'To read a person's mind', reading a graph, reading the lie of the land, etc. In order to understand the processes of learning to read in the strict sense, it is important to see this development within the context of the wider meaning-making – the child's general ability to 'read the world', to interpret and make sense of her experience of living in the human world.

The human world is full of signs and symbols and representations. To 'read' this world in the broadest sense, the child must learn to understand how signs and symbols and presentations relate to real-life experiences. For example, the baby has to learn that the unit of sound 'Dad-dad' means her Daddy and that the figure of Father Christmas means presents. Reading words is just one element in the whole enterprise of learning to read signs and symbols in the world. The general study of this wider 'reading' is called *semiotics*.

Kress (1997), as a semiotician, offers this broader view of literacy which he argues is future-orientated. The child is, as we have acknowledged, an active meaning-maker of both spoken and written language, and Kress expands this notion with the claim that she is also a transformer of language in that meaning-making. He claims the active transformative language work in which the child engages needs to be recognised and harnessed by the educational system so that the required aptitudes and abilities can be capitalised upon. By so doing the individual's intellectual functioning can be maximised in order to cope in the computerised world of the day after tomorrow. He says:

> *We are, it seems, entering a new age of the image, a new age of hieroglyphics; and our school system is not prepared for this at all. Children live in the new world of communication, and on the whole seem to find little problem with it.*

(Kress, 1997, p. xvii)

The ways children arrive at meaning

Kress continues with reference to his own publication:

> *The main points of this book are:*
>
> (a) *We cannot understand how children find their way into print unless we understand the principles of their meaning-making.*
>
> (b) *Children make meaning in an absolute plethora of ways, with an absolute plethora of means, in two, three and four dimensions.*
>
> (c) *Different ways of making meaning involve different kinds of bodily engagement with the world – that is, not just sight as with writing, or hearing as with speech, but touch, smell, taste, feel.*
>
> (d) *If we concede that speech and writing give rise to particular forms of thinking, then we should ask whether touch, taste, smell, feel, also give rise to their specific forms of thinking.*
>
> (e) *In our thinking, subconsciously or consciously, in our feelings, we constantly translate from one medium to another. This ability, and this fact of synaesthesia is essential for humans to understand the world. It is the basis of all metaphor, and of much of our most significant innovation. We may want to foster rather than suppress this activity.*
>
> (f) *In the new communicational and economic world, it may well be that all of these will be essential requirements for culturally, socially, economically,* **humanly** *productive and fulfilling lives.*

(Kress, 1997, p. xviii)

Children, Kress maintains, 'read' text from a broad, rich perspective of the world and its sign-making which is culturally driven, they 'read' or interpret texts as entire structures incorporating within that act the illustrations, the layout, the particular typeface and graphics as a whole and then imbue it with meaning. The evidence cited for this theory is that children 'write' or sign-make in a multi-modal way, using objects such as pillows, boxes, toys, as well as the conventional tools of pens, pencils, paint, felt pens, paper, card, and waste materials, in order to express or as Kress puts it 'design and represent' meaning. Within this thesis, he makes little or no distinction between writing and drawing, and broadens drawing/writing to include model- (sign-) making in three and four dimensions. He implies that distinctions of terminology are not helpful but only hinder the primary teacher/observing adult in the vital role of promoting the further imaginative and cognitive development of this extraordinary and active meaning-maker.

This broader view of literacy is included here to add further weight to the theme of this chapter – the impressive power of the child's intellect. Simultaneously, Kress suggests that learning to read involves the pre-schooler in interpreting and using symbols and signs that encompass images, in addition to conventional print. This necessitates the child getting to grips with iconic representation as well as the symbolic representation of spoken language.

These terms, along with 'enactive', derive from Bruner (1966), and they indicate the three modes of representing our knowledge of the world to ourselves.

- In the *enactive mode*, we know how to do something, for example, to tie our shoelaces, catch a ball, say the alphabet.
- The *iconic mode* is the ability to image, to imagine, to visualise, to use mental maps, etc. That is, there is a spatial resemblance between the mental or physical image and the referent. Thus, a map iconically resembles the geography it represents.
- The *symbolic* or *linguistic mode* is much more abstract and removed from appearances. There is nothing about language, or musical, or mathematical, or scientific notions that resemble what they represent. The word 'dog' is no more like a dog than is the word 'cat'. But the rules for operating with symbolic representation, for example, grammar, makes symbolic representation very flexible and conceptually rich. For example, it enables us to have ideas like 'iconic' and 'symbolic'!

And, as Kress says, young children, on the whole, operate within these different worlds very well.

GETTING TO GRIPS WITH CONVENTIONAL TEXT

The refined, if by comparison more narrowly conventional, understanding of alphabetic symbols and how they work, which is the focus of this volume, develops through the sharing of books and stories, and the exposure to instructions, diagrams and manuals which occurs somewhat later through purposeful encounters with print. It is these print experiences that Yetta Goodman (1991) describes as being the metaphorical soil in which 'the three major roots of literacy with smaller branches within it' grow.

The roots of literacy

The roots, or understandings, of literacy, according to Goodman, are:

1 *The functions and forms that the literacy events serve;*
2 *The use of oral language about written language, which is part of the literacy event and reflects society's values and attitudes toward literacy;*
3 *Conscious awareness about literacy, including its functions, forms and context.*

(Goodman, 1991, p. 136)

Functions and forms of literacy

An awareness of the differing functions and forms of literacy (Goodman, 1991) develops in much the same way that the modes of spoken language are used, copied and re-invented to meet a particular purpose. Children observe and imbue names, signs, directions, logos (often associated with food and drink, for example Cadbury's, Coca Cola and, of course, the ubiquitous MacDonald's!) with meaning. These are context- and culturally-bound and often highly specific to the individual child. The Christmas tree with its mound of tantalising presents invites the pre-schooler to scrutinise gift tags in anticipation.

An appreciation of the features of connected text is dependent upon the opportunity to experience books, stories, letters and cards, and varies considerably from child to child, but it is rare for children to enter school without any understanding of how print and books work (this is expanded upon in Chapter 4). Many children arrive with a vast store of informal knowledge which can be capitalised upon with great benefit as the new pupil learns to read conventionally (Riley, 1996). As with the acquisition of spoken language (see Chapter 1), the role of the adult is the key to the rate of progress achieved in literacy. The quality of the interaction the child encounters as she shares a favourite book over many re-readings scaffolds her understanding, to a greater or lesser extent, into a flexible response to the text. This mutually satisfying sharing of books has the potential to enhance deeper and deeper understanding of the nature of the symbolic system of written language.

An intellectual grasp of writing also develops through living within a literate society and children gradually make the distinction between drawing and writing as they experiment with mark-making of various kinds and for many different purposes. Children, if encouraged by a supply of mark-making tools and tempting paper of various types, colour and size, draw and paint in order to represent their world to themselves and others. The drawing then needs to be labelled, expanded upon with an explanation and, most important of all, for the maker to be identified by name for posterity. For example:

> This boat is a model of the one that Simon was given for his birthday. He made it with Gopal from a box, a smarties tube and glue.

This activity will be supported with talk about writing and drawing and the use of various implements with increasing knowledge, accuracy and definition.

Use of oral language to discuss written language

Pre-school children become able to talk about reading and writing as their understanding develops and they become conscious of the way that other members of a literate society use oral language about written language. Metalinguistic words such as 'pencil', 'felt pen', 'read', 'write', 'book', 'page', 'story' and 'letter' are all connected with the literate act and support the developing concept of what it is to be literate.

CASE STUDY

Developing conceptual understanding of literacy

My grandson had a wooden jigsaw puzzle of his name and at 18 months loved to make and remake it in order to cry triumphantly 'Benjamin' as the last piece was put in place. Before the last letter completed the puzzle it remained merely a jigsaw and not *his* own name.

'What does this say?' 3-year-olds frequently ask pointing to print. At 4, Benjamin was intrigued and slightly irritated when an adult chose to read the Sunday *continued...*

newspapers rather than join him in a game. 'Why don't you say it?' he asked, obviously comparing this silent reading with his own oral reading of text at school and at bedtime. Before this slow-witted adult could formulate a coherent reply, he added 'I know, you are just thinking it!'

These examples indicate a progression with the developing notion of literacy and with the concept of what it is to be literate. Young children recognise the power of literacy to develop thought and also the unshakeable belief that they, too, will be readers and writers one day soon.

What activities can be provided in the early years setting to support children with this developing understanding of literacy and what it involves?

Conscious knowledge about literacy

The facility to use spoken language in connection with written language moves the child forward into a more 'conscious knowledge about literacy' (Goodman, 1991). This more conscious awareness is demonstrated in many ways, for example, with the realisation that print is unchanging and always stands for the same piece of spoken language. Anyone who has read to a 3-year-old will recognise this especially if she or he has been castigated for turning two pages at once so missing out a section of a favourite story. The development of the **concepts about print** will follow (see Chapter 3) and, later still, the vital and essential understanding of the alphabet as a symbolic system and its flexible representation of the sounds of speech. This understanding represents an intellectual leap and is crucial for progress along the path of literacy. It can be encouraged by direct teaching, but can only genuinely develop through the prolonged exposure to meaningful encounters with print and texts alongside a supportive adult during the pre-school years.

concepts about print
the concepts that children develop about how print works to represent spoken language, which can be demonstrated by their reading behaviours

The top-down processing skills

Capitalising on the proven meaning-making strategies of learning to talk, reading initially is well described by Goodman (1973) as a 'psycho-linguistic guessing game'. Young children mimic the experienced reader as they demonstrate 'reading-like' behaviours of retelling the story, turning the pages, pointing to words and matching them to a unit of spoken language. The approximation denotes a grasp of the narrative form, often the use of literary language and capitalising on picture cues to prompt memory. The lively retelling of the story or the experimental 'FR-O-O-O-ST-IIIIIES' when pointing to the print on the cereal packet denotes a reworking of the meaning in a recreation that parallels the earlier experimentation with spoken language through conversational exchange.

CASE STUDY

The reworking of texts

Holdaway (1982) uses two transcripts of children reworking the same text as they behave like readers at very different stages of literacy development.

'Damion, age 2 years, retrieving *Are you my Mother?*:

Text	Responses
4 The egg jumped. "Oh!Oh!" said the motherbird. "My baby will be here! He will want to eat."	Ow! Ow! A mummy bird baby here. Someping a eat ("a" used throughout to replace "to" and "for")
6 "I must get something for my baby to eat"	Must baby bird a [i.e. "to"] eated Dat way went. Fly a gye
she said "I will be back."	
So away she went.	

Lisa-Jane, 4.0 years, from the same book:

Text	Responses
34 The kitten and the hen were not his mother. The dog and the cow were not his mother. Did he have a mother?	So the pussy wasn't his mother. The hen wasn't his mother. The dog wasn't his mother. The cow wasn't his mother. And the baby bird said "Did I have a mother?" and he DID!
36 "I did have a mother." said the baby bird. "I know I did. I have to find her. I will. I WILL!"	What a sad face. That one says Did he have a mother. Did he have a mother? He DID!'

(Holdaway, 1982, p. 296)

A great deal more than the accurate comprehension of the text is demonstrated by these children, as each one uses the appropriate level of spoken language available to him/her. Understanding of the whole story (global context) is the starting point, accompanied with sentence-by-sentence retrieval. In addition, there is awareness of the deep structure of the language, its patterns and cadence, as the meaning and the narrative are recreated with fresh enjoyment.

1 This kind of reworking of text is an important part of becoming literate. What opportunities can we offer nursery and reception children to retell favourite stories?
2 How might the adult help a child to rework a story? By making a book with her?

Recollection of the text plays a role as the children start to use **top-down processing** (see Figure I.1, page x) of text to anticipate words. This term describes the processing of print that includes the skills that rely on prediction to read the text.

- One type of predictive **cue** is the use of the meaning as it is embedded in the whole context or, put another way, knowing the complete story through previous readings and discussion and through the prompt of the illustrations. This is known as *predicting through the global context*.
- Another predictive cue is the use of **semantics** – the meaning within a sentence as it unfolds.
- The third predictive cue is the use of **syntax** – the grammatical structure indicated mainly, and particularly initially, in the word order of a sentence or clause.

First, children learn to use all the predictive cues available in a text. They then move to the next level of literacy development as they recognise a few highly distinctive individual words. This is achieved through the particular shape of some of the frequently repeated words and later still by some of the letters, and the so-called **bottom-up processing** skills are brought into play. (This aspect of print processing is discussed fully in Chapter 3.)

top-down processing
processing that informs the identification of words from the context by anticipating what the text is likely to say

cues
the clues a reader uses in identifying words and determining meanings

semantics
meanings – both the meaning of individual words and the meaning of complete texts

syntax
grammar – the ways that words go together (word order) to make sentences

bottom-up processing
the aspect of the reading process concerned with identifying the words on the page

CASE STUDY

Making meaning with text

This example of a 6-year-old reading a text shows how, by her errors or miscues, her developing print-processing ability is utilising the prediction cues of context, semantics and syntax to decode words that she does not yet have stored in her visual memory or her sight vocabulary. There are several ways of recognising a word at sight. Very young children, for example, even before they have begun to learn the alphabet, can rote-learn a sight vocabulary logographically. As adults, we recognise nearly all the words we encounter orthographically as sight-words. That is, we know them as fully processed and over-learned spelling patterns.

'Nadia, age 6, reading *Mrs Wishy Washy*, Nelson Storychest:

Text	Responses
2 "Oh, lovely mud," said the cow,	"Oh, lovely mud," said the cow,
3 and she jumped in it.	and she jumped in it.
4 "Oh, lovely mud," said the pig,	"Oh, what mud," said the **big** – self-corrected – pig,
5 and he rolled in it.	and he rolled in it.

continued...

6 "Oh, lovely mud" said the duck,	"Oh, **look** – *self-corrected* – **what** mud," said the duck,
7 and she paddled in it.	and she **jumped** in it.
8. Along came Mrs Wishy Washy	Along came Mrs Wishy Washy
9 "Just look at you," look at you she screamed.	**What did** – *self-corrected* – she **shouted**.'

(Riley, 1996, p. 124)

emboldened text = miscues or errors

Nadia is working hard to process this text and is relying heavily on her memory and prediction skills. She has a good knowledge of the story and its meaning. She has memorised some of the patterned phrases – 'Oh lovely mud,' and this is remembered on page 2, but by page 4. it has become 'Oh, *what* mud,' which makes perfect sense. Then 'and she paddled in it' becomes 'and she *jumped* in it' by page 7 partly memorised from page 3 but making acceptable sense semantically and syntactically.

Active processing and using to the full the limited strategies available to her in her creation of the text is shown most clearly on page 9. Nadia reads '*What did. . .*' and then self-corrects as she gets to the 'at you' realising 'What did at you' is semantically and syntactically inappropriate and she then re-reads it as '*look at you she shouted*' using sense well, although indicating that she has little graphophonic (letter–sound) cueing ability developed as yet. There are a couple of instances that indicate an embryonic awareness of the connection that print represents a sound with her *big/pig* confusion on page 4. and perhaps with the *look/lovely* miscue which may have been triggered by the *lo. . .* at the beginning of the words. A very positive strategy demonstrated by Nadia is the self-correction of her reading as she checks and cross-checks for meaning and appropriateness. Her pulling together of the sense as she processes the text (albeit with limited use of cueing strategies and an over-reliance on top-down processing) shows an important advance in reading development.

1   What does Nadia need to know in order to progress?
2   What kinds of activity will help her to develop print–sound awareness? Look at the suggestions at the end of Chapter 3.

The ability of the brain to fill the gaps and to make sense from the cues of context, demonstrates the guessing-game nature of reading (particularly in the very early stages) and this is illustrated helpfully by the birthday card shown in Figure 2.1a. Without the picture (Figure 2.1b), it is very hard to fathom the words.

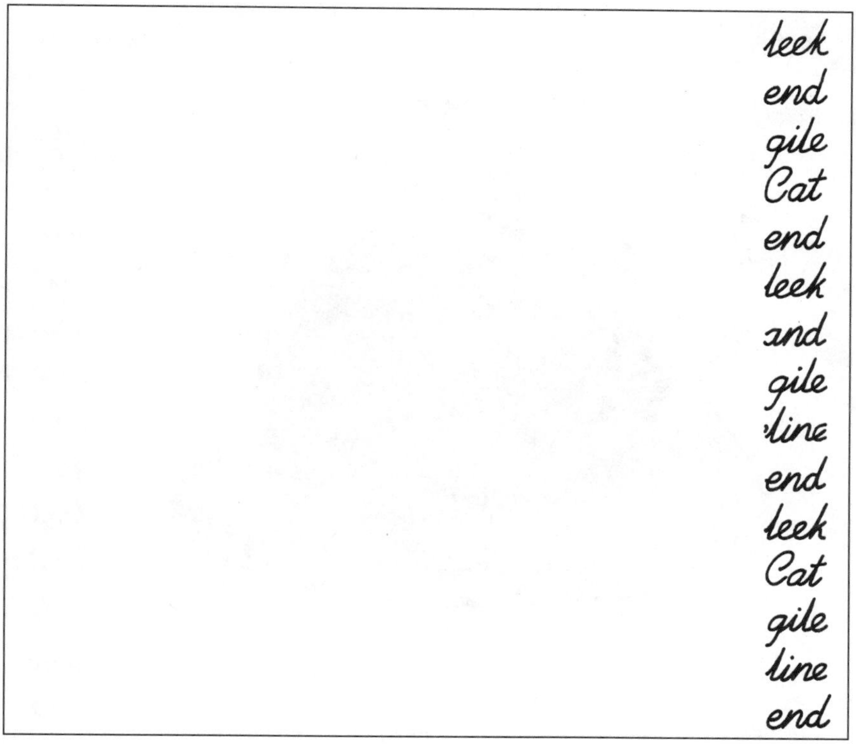

leek
end
gile
Cat
end
leek
and
gile
line
end
leek
Cat
gile
line
end

Figure 2.1a
The role of prediction in reading. Can you read the words and parts of words? Now look at Figure 2.1b

Holdaway (1982) asserts that the examples given earlier of Damion and Lisa-Jane recreating their loved stories has links in the way that spoken language is learned. Complex human skills are practised with an approximation of the mature manifestation of the skill. Appropriate processes and strategies provide the foundation for practice and refinement.

Holdaway is clear on the most productive strategies that lead to success for the novice reader:

- *A deep, meaning-centred drive.*
- *Confirmatory and corrective self-monitoring by which output is constantly compared with sound models in prior experiences.*
- *Risk-taking by approximation and trial backed by these sound strategies of self monitoring.*

(Holdaway, 1982, p. 279)

This view of reading is confirmed by Clay who eloquently defines reading as 'a message-gaining, problem-solving activity, which increases in power and flexibility the more it is practised' (1979).

Figure 2.1b
The role of prediction in reading

leek
end
gile
Cat
end
leek
and
gile
line
end
leek
Cat
gile
line
end

The thorny issue for the early years teacher is how this informal way of scaffolding the child's learning whilst reading and working on text, typically in the one child with one adult situation, can be transformed into practice for the early years classroom.

Implications for practice

Firstly, the teacher needs to be aware of ways in which a child might be encouraged to use the most helpful of reading strategies (Goodman, 1972, 1973, 1976) to promote positive reading behaviours. For fluent reading to develop the young child needs strategies that will enable her to:

- sample
- predict
- confirm or self-correct.

Sample
The novice reader needs to sample (or focus on) effectively those details of meaning and print which inform (*or confirm or correct*) a prediction about a word. This means the child should be encouraged to separate out the most helpful features of print in order to identify

a word. The adult might point out the likelihood of a word being what it is from earlier reading of the text or from the illustration, or a word previously encountered or one that is known from another context. In order to sample the child will use:

- **sight vocabulary**
- salient print features of words.

Predict
The child learns to predict text based on expectations formed by experience. The reader brings a knowledge of semantic, syntactic and graphophonic (letter–sound) expectations to the text. These become more refined as the child progresses. Context and picture cues are an important aid, but it is the analysis of letters and their sounds and the shape and look of words that reduces uncertainty (see Chapter 3) about a word and turns predicting into accurate decoding. Look again at Figures 2.1a and 2.1b which demonstrate this.

Confirm or self-correct
The child needs constantly to confirm the accuracy of the predictions through attention to the meaning and the orthography (features of print), and if inaccurate, to self-correct. As this ability becomes perfected the information needed is reduced. As the cueing strategies become established the processing of connected text becomes more efficient and fast. The appropriate cues are rapidly selected and cross-checked, **miscues** identified, re-reading may occur and certainty is confirmed.

SUPPORTING THE DEVELOPMENT OF POSITIVE READING STRATEGIES

Every time the child reads, the teacher needs to monitor sensitively and informally the strategies the reader is able to use and to develop explicitly – the ability to sample (or select appropriate visual information), to predict, to confirm and self-correct. This can be done by drawing attention clearly to the most appropriate cues, building first on what the pupil knows of spoken language, then to what she knows of print and the specific text.

The aim is to encourage independence by praising useful strategies at a level of specificity to support learning, for example, 'Well done, you thought that out! You remembered that word from yesterday/ the word rhymes with ___/You knew it started with *bl* not *br* . . .'. If the adult observes what the child is *actually doing* when reading this will indicate what the reader knows and understands. This then can inform decisions about future teaching.

sight vocabulary
words that an individual can recognise at sight without having to decode

miscue
an error or mistake in reading a word, resulting from processing or taking into account only a part of the information available

Teaching to support print awareness

The building of a sight vocabulary enables the child to have a store of rapidly recognised words for use in both reading and writing. It encourages print awareness, which in turn, facilitates speedy print processing and automatic recognition of patterns and letter groupings and the sounds they represent. The following activities are fundamental and integral to all literacy teaching in the early years classroom:

- extensive reading of many different kinds of high quality texts
- frequent transfer of spoken language into written language in meaningful and interesting activities and situations (see the discussion of the Language Experience Approach in Chapter 1)
- children writing for themselves and others using familiar words and phrases with 'invented spelling' (or developmental writing)
- beginning readers need to see and be encouraged to focus upon familiar words and phrases in different and varied contexts, for example, notices, books, cards, letters, in writing for them and by them.

invented spelling
spelling words phonically using emerging print/sound knowledge; works within the alphabetic system; supports the development of bottom-up processing

More detailed teaching approaches to support the development of the literacy process through focused teaching of the constituent skills are to be found in Chapter 3.

Teaching to support effective prediction skills

The child needs to be encouraged to make use of global prediction cues in order to predict words accurately. Firstly, teachers can encourage this ability by choosing material of the appropriate level of difficulty. This includes consideration of whether the concepts and vocabulary in the text are within the child's experience. The important point here is that teachers need be knowledgeable about the books that they use in order to maximise the learning opportunities for their pupils. Secondly, introducing the child to the book before sharing it is of value. This is discussed fully later in this chapter.

Teachers can introduce the reader to the ideas and words contained in a book in preparation for reading the text itself. A shared or guided (used with a group of readers working with multiple copies of the same text) first reading of a book builds on the expectations the child has of the story, of the language structures and the child's knowledge of syntax – for example, whether the word will be a verb, whether a noun will be singular or plural from the determiners such as subject/verb agreement. This makes explicit to the novice reader the processing of the text that she will soon be doing.

Teaching to support confirmation and self-correction skills

When a prediction about a word is made, the reader needs to confirm the accuracy. As the child's repertoire of strategies develops, increasingly minimal information is selected from the available cues and is cross-checked. If uncertainty remains, self-correction is needed and additional cues will be used and considered. For example, having failed to solve the problem by looking only at the initial letter–sound, the child may look at the ending of the word to further confirm accuracy, and meaning is called upon to further check the sense by re-reading the sentence. This is called cross-checking. In the early stages of reading, children often need encouragement to use a full range of their meaning-making strategies to read unfamiliar words.

Teachers can support the developing use of strategies to confirm and cross-check predictions by making sure that:

- both the concepts and the language of the text are at an appropriate level of difficulty so that cross-checking does not have to occur so frequently that the meaning is lost. A book is too hard for a child if she is unable to read more than 10 per cent of the text, i.e. if one word in 10 is too difficult for her to work out. See Chapter 5 for discussion of appropriate match of book to child
- the responsibility for confirming the predictions is given to the child. Questions such as 'How did you know that was the right word?' (sometimes at the end of the piece so that neither fluency nor motivation are lost) and 'Does that make sense?' prompt and stimulate positive reading strategies
- the child is encouraged to use her awareness of the cues available, to learn how to make decisions about the most useful cues on different occasions. This realisation has to be achieved for meaning to be effectively and speedily reconstructed.

Gradually, as the child becomes more competent, the cueing strategies employed are fully integrated and become mutually supportive so that the reader has what Clay (1991) describes as 'the construction of inner control'. Successful readers are able to make instantaneous decisions of sampling (selecting) the salient features of text, predicting and then confirming the prediction, by appropriate, fast and economical cross-checking.

Once the child can integrate all cueing strategies, she will improve every time she reads. See Chapter 3 for detailed discussion of the cueing strategies of bottom-up processing.

There are three categories of cues, corresponding to the three sources of information available to the reader, namely:

- semantic cues resulting from the context of meaning
- syntactic cues resulting from the grammatical context
- graphophonic cues derived from the print on the page.

In reading, the child needs to co-ordinate information from all three kinds of cue. For example, a child reading 'It was raining, so he put up his. . .' may anticipate from the grammar that he needs a noun, he may anticipate something like 'collar' or 'umbrella' from the context of meaning, and may decode the first or last letters of the word 'umbrella' in the text. Successfully integrating these three cues he reads 'umbrella'.

Teaching to support the child to integrate the cueing strategies

A child with few decoding strategies at her disposal will rely too heavily on a narrow repertoire, and be permanently struggling to make sense of the text, except with very familiar, well known and favourite books. Skilled monitoring of the child's reading through use of observation and recording techniques such as the running reading record (see Chapter 5) will help the teacher to identify precisely what the reader can do and which strategies need to be developed.

As the teacher is observing the child working on text, it is important that:

- the teacher does not intervene too early
- the child is encouraged to show independent problem-solving or prediction using context and syntax
- meaning and sense are the first cues for confirming and cross-checking
- re-reading pulls together the available information to make the sentence (or phrase) whole and clarify meaning
- the child is then directed to strategies using the visual information namely grapheme–phoneme (letter–sound) correspondence and the shape or 'look' of the word.

These principles underpin all teaching of reading in the early stages of literacy with both individuals and groups.

Activities to develop literacy

The following activities are designed to develop the ability to sample (select) print appropriately, to predict and to confirm the meaning of text.

Reading to children

Reading to children may take place with the whole class, with smaller groups of children at the same reading level or with mixed level groups.

Reading stimulating, exciting stories and high-quality non-fiction books to children is fundamental to any literacy programme. Teachers are able to use these opportunities to share the mutual enjoyment of a story and the fascination with new ideas to reinforce the fact that:

- reading is an important, culturally required tool
- there is a delight in hearing literary language
- children's literature offers awareness of a wider world not yet experienced and has the potential to promote intellectual, moral and emotional development
- hearing stories develops the spoken English of bilingual learners.

Reading books and stories to young children using enlarged texts explicitly promotes understanding of the conventions of print.

Shared reading

Shared reading may take place with either the whole class or with smaller groups of children. It involves the active role of participation by the child whilst enjoying class stories, large texts (either commercially- or class-produced) and written poems. The principle began with Holdaway in the 1960s and emulated the intuitive, pre-school book-sharing of adult and child, in which the child is supported into positive reading behaviours by the adult. This technique is now one of the enshrined approaches in the National Literacy Strategy *Framework for Teaching* (DfEE, 1998).

It is well documented that this experience is a powerful learning approach (Ninio and Bruner, 1978) and can be of great value in the hands of the experienced teacher. Whether in a one-to-one situation, in a small group or whole-class setting, the child is not only learning the content and knowledge involved in the story or book under discussion, but is also fulfilling the following learning objectives:

- the conventions about print
- familiarisation with conventions of punctuation
- 'interrogation' of illustrations and text
- the use of prediction as cueing strategy
- one-to-one correspondence or the matching of a spoken word to the relevant written word
- close attention to visual details of letters and groups of letters
- a sight vocabulary of high-frequency words
- a familiarisation with rhythmic and repetitive language.

The National Literacy Strategy *Framework for Teaching* (DfEE, 1998) suggests that this activity should occur frequently – four or five times a week in reception and Year 1 classes – in addition to the reading of a daily story. The aim of shared reading is to provide support for the novice reader so that she is able to enjoy the material that she is not yet sufficiently proficient to tackle alone. In addition, shared reading develops the important strategies of sampling (selecting), predicting, confirming and self-correcting for use on text when reading independently. The power of a good story is crucial to withstand repeated collaborative readings.

Introduction to a text
This should be done with a group of same level readers.

Book introductions are a valuable way to prepare children to be able to predict the text. They know the story and are familiar with the vocabulary before attempting to read independently. The teacher can achieve this by 'tuning in' the children to the title, the characters, the illustrations, and the possible story line *without* revealing the entire plot and so reducing any intrigue that is a strong motivating force. It takes practice to entice the readers into anticipating the delight of the book and also to be informative about it!

Having introduced and then discussed a book, the teacher will invite responses and comments on the illustrations. The first reading of the book enables confusions to be clarified, misunderstandings to be reconciled and prediction skills to be reinforced. The children's knowledge of the world and language are drawn upon to predict words and forthcoming events. As children become more confident and competent, considerations of graphophonic (letter–sound) associations, shape and length of words can be encouraged in order to confirm or self-correct predictions.

The analysis of the reading task with word-level work should never be allowed to diminish the pleasure of the story. The skilled early years teacher is aware of the strengths and weaknesses of a given group of children and what needs to be taught for later fluent, independent reading. This teacher knows how to teach and reinforce the precise and appropriate understandings at word, sentence and text levels and when to enliven the shared reading of the story at exactly the right pace.

Further sharings of the same book
This should take place with group of same level readers.

Taking care not to destroy all enjoyment in the story, subsequent sharing of the book over the following few days might lead to further teaching activities such as:

- joining in if there is an often repeated refrain, for example, 'Run, run as fast as you can. . .' (*The Gingerbread Man*, traditional tale)
- reading in unison the written refrain from a strip of card in the appropriate place in the story
- reading a commercially-produced enlarged text in unison
- after the sharing of enlarged text, individuals can group-read with multiple copies later
- reading in unison along with the audio-taped version
- after several hearings of the taped version, the text may be attempted independently.

All of these activities rely on the strength of the story and quality of the text to sustain interest. The choice of the text is crucial and it is rare that an enlarged text from a commercial reading scheme has the potential for both pleasure and reading practice.

Summary

We have explored the links between learning to speak and learning to read and write. The links involve similarity in the way that the child:

- **learns to operate in both spoken and written language – her active engagement with the task through personal interest and the desire to communicate and to understand communication**

- **initially uses symbols to reconstruct meaning from text and the way that learning accomplished when learning to talk – approximation of the accurate form precedes perfect production as the reader gradually comes to terms with the complexity of all that is involved.**

The role of the adult in supporting reading progress is crucial, scaffolding the child's attempts to read through:

- **modelling mature reading behaviour**

- **enabling the sampling of text**

- **supporting the prediction of a word**

- **confirming the prediction through the use of the available cues, and correcting miscues.**

Further reading

Clay, M.M. (1991) *Becoming Literate: The Construction of Inner Control,* London: Heinemann
This is a detailed account of early literacy teaching by one of the world's most influential theoreticians.

Holdaway, D. (1979) *Foundations of Literacy*, Gosford, NSW: Scholastic Publications
This is a period piece in a way, but it is interesting to see where many of the ideas now enshrined in the Literacy Hour have come from.

Holdaway, D. (1982) 'Shared book experience: Teaching reading using favourite books', *Theory into Practice*, Vol. XXI, No. 4., pp 293–300
This book provides a magnifying glass look at early literacy development, and is particularly good on the retelling strategies of very young children.

The importance of print and sound awareness 3

When you have read this chapter, you should:

- understand both the similarities in and the differences between learning to speak and learning to read

- be aware of the importance of phonological awareness in learning to read

- be aware that recognising individual letters leads to a grasp of the nature of the alphabetic code, and therefore the links between sounds and letters

- know how teachers can support the development of these skills in their pupils.

Introduction

. . .research indicates that the skilful reader's remarkable ability to recognise printed words derives from a deep and ready knowledge of their composite sequences of letters along with the connections of those spellings to speech and meaning.

(Adams, 1993)

Here Adams is calling upon the huge body of research evidence that redresses the balance of the often quoted claim that reading is a 'psycholinguistic guessing game' (Goodman, 1976). Quite evidently, it is not as straightforward as that. We have seen from the previous chapter that this top-down processing is an important part of the literacy process, but there is another crucial aspect with which the child has to get to grips.

HOW SPOKEN AND WRITTEN LANGUAGE ARE LEARNED

There are similarities between the acquisition of both spoken and written language. The active engagement in the construction of meaning is an essential aspect that is present in both modes of language development; both are used, initially at least, to fulfil immediate and personally satisfying purposes.

Similarities between written and spoken language

There are features that are common both to learning to speak and learning to read. They are as follows.

- The motivation to become involved is gained through the purposefulness of the spoken or written encounters.
- The learning of spoken language is essentially about learning to *mean*, as is learning written language, which draws on the earlier achievement of oracy. Children work out the rules of speech for themselves through interacting with experienced conversationalists and they use this problem-solving ability as they continue to work towards the generation of rules when puzzling out text.
- When interacting with text, children form hypotheses, that is they predict (or anticipate) words through selecting the most productive cues to confirm meaning. These strategies have been learnt through understanding speech.
- Facilitative adults are vital, albeit in different ways, to the successful achievement of competence in both language modes.

Differences between written and spoken language

There are, however, distinct and important differences between oracy and literacy. Purcell-Gates (1996) lists the characteristics of written language. It is used to:

- communicate over time and space. Written language must therefore be shaped so that meaning is conveyed in the absence of a shared physical context between writer and reader. Conversely with conversation there is the support of the situation and presence of the speakers. Meaning is negotiated through gesture and repetition, and confusion can be immediately clarified
- make thoughts and emotions permanent and when writing there is time to express these ideas and feelings precisely. The opportunity exists to re-read in order to establish clarity. This results in vocabulary (for example, literary language such as 'entrance' instead of 'door'), syntax (that is more complex and integrated), and reference conventions being used differently from speaking. We write sentences such as 'There cannot be anyone who, believing this to be true, will continue to purchase cosmetics that have been tested on animals', rather than the spoken version, 'Nobody who knows about the testing of make-up on animals will buy them.'

- accommodate different degrees of involvement between the writer and reader. The impersonal nature of text has to be considered by the writer in order to make the meaning clear.

Also, when learning to use written symbols (to **decode** and **encode**), it is necessary to understand that the writing system is an artificial code. Certainly, this new learning is grafted onto the 'embeddedness' of the previous learning of speech (Donaldson, 1989). In Bielby's (1999) words 'learning to read and write are parasitic on learning to speak' and the many previously acquired skills (see the previous two chapters) can be utilised. This understanding regarding the nature and function of the **alphabetic code** is crucial to successful literacy learning. But it can develop (through opportunities to engage with text and direct teaching) only after the secure establishment of the concept that print has a communicative function and that its use is governed by certain rules and conventions (see Chapter 4).

RECOGNISING THAT THE ALPHABET IS A CODE

Children gradually become literate over many years and through many thousands of exposures to texts and signs. The recognition that the alphabet is a symbolic system that represents the sounds of speech in a written code, and from which the meaning of language can be retrieved, is exciting and life-changing. Research evidence has informed understanding of the mechanisms at work in this journey of discovery, as the child learns that spoken language is represented by written symbols in order to create text.

Before any progress on the path to literacy can be made, the child needs to appreciate, through a wealth of first-hand experience, that a written text is permanent and unchanging. This will occur mainly through books. The development of this understanding is demonstrated by the infuriated appeal to justice when a bed-time story is brought to an end or when a favourite part of the tale left out. Children as young as 3 years old know exactly when they have been short-changed on a much loved re-reading of a story (see Chapters 2 and 4).

After this understanding, awareness of the rules and conventions of print is the next intellectual task for the child to achieve before the complexity of the code-breaking (bottom-up skills) part of the literacy processing can be tackled (see Figure I.1, page x).

decoding
the process of identifying the written word using the **alphabetic code** to determine pronunciation and meaning

encoding
the process of representing the spoken word in writing using the symbols of the **alphabetic code**

alphabetic code
a system of symbols representing the constituent sounds within words, for **encoding** the spoken word and **decoding** the written word

The importance of print and sound processing skills

Primary teachers need to be aware of crucial research findings.

- Firstly, there is substantial evidence that young children find segmenting spoken words into discrete units of sound very difficult.
- Secondly, the ability to read and write successfully and fluently depends upon segmenting spoken words, albeit after the individual has recognised the wider and more global understandings of the purpose and nature of literacy (see Chapters 2 and 4).

Becoming an effective user of the alphabetic system is dependent upon the accurate segmenting of words into the constituent **phonemes** (which is known as **phonemic segmentation**) and then the ability to map the sounds onto symbols. Phonemes are the minimal sound segments that constitute a spoken word, allowing it to be recognised. Change a phoneme and the word is changed. Phonemes roughly correspond to the individual letter and digraph (and other letter combination) sounds – thus, 'patch' corresponds to the three phonemes in patch thus, p/+/a/+/ch. By changing the middle phoneme to /i/, it becomes /pitch/.

This is only part of the process of becoming literate, but it is an essential part and without it the child is denied accuracy.

Difficulties in phonemic segmentation

Primary teachers have a vital role to play in enabling children to develop **phonological awareness** and, unfortunately for both parties, it is a slow skill to develop!

The research evidence regarding the difficulties that children have making explicit phonological judgements is now well known in the field of psychology. Bruce (1964) found that 5–9-year-old children were not able to remove a phoneme from a given word, such as the 'n' in 'sand', in a 'subtraction' task. Liberman *et al.* (1974) gave 4-, 5- and 6-year-old children a 'tapping' task. They taught the children to tap out either the **syllables** or the phonemes of a word presented to them by the researcher. A syllable is a unit of sound centred on a vowel sound, which is a vocal pulse of energy. This vowel sound may, and need not, be accompanied by consonant sounds preceding and following it. A word must contain at least one syllable.

This the children found very difficult also. They found the syllable tapping task easier than the phoneme task, but the 5-year-olds simply could not learn to discriminate between the different phonemes within even short, regular words.

---

phoneme
the smallest unit of sound in a word; a phoneme may be represented by one, two, three or four letters, e.g. **to**, sh**oe**, thr**ough**

phonemic segmentation
the skill of distinguishing the individual phonemes in words, e.g. the four phonemes in 'fox'

phonological awareness
the perceptual alertness to the constituent sounds within words, ranging from alertness to rhymes and alliteration to distinguishing the individual phonemes

syllable
the phonological unit in a word that centres on a vowel sound, together with its associated consonants

It seemed therefore that pre-literate children find breaking words into units of sound very hard and that breaking words into syllables is easier than identifying phonemes. Basing their work on the same principle, Treiman and Baron (1981) replicated this study. Children were asked to set out counters for the syllables that they could hear in a word in one case, and the phonemes in another. This study showed again that young children find the phoneme discrimination task problematic. Does it matter? And what is the evidence that this skill is essential to learning to read?

PHONOLOGICAL AWARENESS AND LEARNING TO READ

Research findings do seem to indicate that there is a very strong relationship between children's ability in making phonological judgements and their success in learning to read. Over the last two decades studies have indicated this from three different sources of evidence.

Firstly, one category of investigation showed that there is a very strong relationship between the ability of individuals to break words into phonemes and their progress in learning to read. This relationship holds even when the effect of intelligence is taken into account (Stanovich *et al.*, 1984a and 1984b; Tunmer *et al.*, 1988).

Secondly, other studies have shown that children who are backward in reading also function poorly on **grapheme**–phoneme correspondence tasks. Graphemes are the alphabetic representations of phonemes – thus 'rough' represents the three phonemes /r/+/u/+/ff/, and 'cat' represents the three phonemes of /cat/. Grapheme–phoneme correspondence refers to the regularities that constitute phonics. This ability is tested with experiments that use pseudo-words (for example, 'wem' and 'tugwump') that the child could not possibly have seen before and therefore could not have stored in her memory bank, or sight vocabulary, of known words (Frith and Snowling, 1983).

grapheme
the alphabetic representation of a phoneme, e.g. 'rough' represents the three phonemes /r/+/u/+/ff/

In the third category of enquiry there are the intervention studies in which pre-school children were given extra phonological experience in breaking words up into their constituent phonemes and also building words from phonemes (Lundberg *et al.*, 1988). In Lundberg's follow-up study it seemed that the children who had received the extra phonological training did indeed learn to read more successfully than those pupils who had received as much attention from adults but not the extra phonological training.

What facilitates the development of phonological awareness?

Since being able to segment words into sound units of various types (but crucially, into phonemes) is essential for effective progress in literacy, it is obviously important that primary teachers, particularly early years teachers, know how to enable pupils to develop phonological awareness.

The appreciation of the alphabetic code

This is a paradoxical issue. It seems that individuals learn how to break words into their sounds *through* learning to read and yet it has been shown that this skill is crucial for the successful acquisition of literacy. A child who has not made the connection that words are made up of sounds and that these sounds map onto letters and groups of letters in various combinations has not grasped the principle of the alphabetic code. She is then forced into two main strategies for decoding text. Firstly, relying on its distinctive shape to recall a word and, secondly, to back up this strategy by confirming accuracy through predicting the word from the context (see Chapter 2). Both of these strategies are useful, but they become truly effective only when complemented with the strategy of grapheme–phoneme (letter–sound) correspondence.

The findings of research show that illiterate adults have similar difficulties with separating words into phonemes as has been demonstrated with pre-literate children (Morais *et al.*, 1979; 1986). This seminal work indicates that competent and functioning, but illiterate, adults do not naturally develop this very specific, and it would appear, literacy-dependent ability. It seems that people become aware of phonemes when they use the alphabet to read and write. Interesting and complementary work provides further explanation of this issue as to whether phonemic awareness is facilitated by the use of the alphabet or being literate. Read *et al.* (1986) have undertaken research with individuals who have learned to read and write with a non-alphabetic script, such as traditional Chinese, a logographic script in which logograms represent whole words. These studies replicated the work of Morais *et al.* on groups of adults, some of whom were literate in an alphabetic script and some in a logographic script. The results show that individuals who are literate, but in a non-alphabetic script, have enormous difficulty with phonemic segmentation.

This point is developed later in Chapter 7 when addressing the issue of bilingual children learning to read. The task for this group of children is facilitated or hindered by whether or not their first language has an alphabetic script. This adds further weight to the evidence of the necessity for individuals to operate in an alphabetic system in order to come to understand fully that it is a code. This supports the paradox discussed earlier – the ability to segment phonemes is essential in order to become literate in an alphabetic script and in order to be able to segment phonemes, an individual has to be functional in a script with an the alphabetic code! Unfortunately, it is not even as simple (or complex!) as that because the reader also has to be able to build up sounds into words and so access meaning.

Rhyme and rime

If phonemic segmentation is hard for young, pre-literate children, are there other units of sound that are easier for them both to identify and discriminate between? The answer is yes. Pre-school children are adept at playing with and detecting sound at the level of **rhyme** and alliteration (Dowker, 1989; Bryant *et al.*, 1989). Whilst there is a wide variation between 3- and 4-year-old children in their ability to distinguish words that rhyme from words that do not, it is clear that this sound unit is easier for them to hear and sort out than syllables or phonemes. There is also evidence that being able to identify rhyme at nursery school is a very good predictor of early success with reading at school (Bradley and Bryant, 1983). The way this works has been much debated. It seems odd that being able to detect rhyme is useful if the main and most important goal of phonological awareness is to be able to phonemically segment so that accurate grapheme–phoneme (letter–sound) correspondences can be made when encoding and decoding print. Being able to hear and discriminate rhyme is a different skill, it would appear, and is layered with a myriad of complexities relating to aural and visual rhymes and the vagaries of English spelling rules.

rhyme
words containing the same **rime** in their final **syllable** are said to rhyme, e.g. acro**bat**/**chat**, **down**/**clown**; however, words are said to rhyme also when they have the same *sound* in the final syllable, e.g. bear/hair – these are known as *near rhymes* or *aural rhymes*

The point appears to be that phonological awareness develops in stages. First children are able to distinguish rhyme, then syllables and later still phonemes in words (see Figure 3.1). If rhyme is the first sound unit that young children are able to detect, it is useful because it demonstrates that phonological awareness has begun to develop and can then be built upon further.

Another reason why rhyme may be so useful in the early stages of learning to read is that the ability to detect rhyme is a short step from the ability to identify the sound units of **onset** and **rime** to which the identification of rhyme is linked. It has been shown that it is important for a child to be able to appreciate rime (Goswami and Bryant, 1990). For example, to realise what the rimes of '1-*ook*', 'b-*ook*' and 'sh-*ook*' have in common, namely both a sound element and a related visual element, in other words the spelling pattern, is

onset
beginning **phoneme** of word/**syllable**, precedes the vowel sound (the **rime**), e.g., **b**-at or **br**-at

rime
the vowel sound and any subsequent consonant sounds of a word/**syllable**, following the **onset**, e.g., b-**at** and br-**at**

Figure 3.1
*A causal-developmental
theory of reading*

1) Preschool rhyming and alliteration

Awareness of linguistic units of onsets and rimes

Early reading development (rime analogies)

2) Reading and spelling experience

Increasing specification of phonemes

3) Reading   Spelling

(Increasing convergence of strategies)

(Goswami 1995)

to begin to realise that spellings and sounds relate in a regular and specific way. In particular, it is to realise that it is possible to work out new words on this basis, words such as 'took', 'cook', 'crook', etc. This ability also then enables the distinction between dissimilar onsets of 't. . .' and 'c. . .' and 'cr. . .'. This awareness is not only well within the grasp of early readers, it also becomes another cueing strategy for decoding when they need to read an unknown word but one that has a familiar rime. Goswami and Bryant (1990) found that even very young children can read 'l-*ake*' because they are able to read 't-*ake*' in another situation. That is, they are able to use the analogy of the **intrasyllabic unit** of the rime of a word to decode accurately a new word not currently in their sight vocabulary. Their significance is that they are the smallest phonological units that children seem spontaneously to be alert to, without being prompted by adults or by being taught alphabet letter sounds.

intrasyllabic unit
a unit of onset plus rime
within (intra-) a **syllable**

ORTHOGRAPHIC AWARENESS

If anybody, not necessarily a teacher or someone connected with primary education, were asked to make a list of the most important aspects involved with learning to read and write, high on that list would surely be the necessity for a level of visual discrimination and perception. It probably would be agreed that a novice reader needs, first, sufficiently developed visual discrimination in order to detect the differences (and some of the differences *are* very slight and mainly due to orientation, for example, p, q, b, d) between the 26 printed symbols of the alphabet; and second, the ability to perceive and remember words as wholes and to attach a meaning to the remembered shape of the word.

However, as has been discussed previously, the business of getting to grips with literacy is not as visual an activity as one might innocently imagine. The importance of the ability to hear the constituent sounds in individual words in order to read fluently in an alphabetic script has been addressed in detail. Clearly though, the sounds once identified and segmented, or separated, have then to be mapped onto recalled symbols or letters. This is called **orthographic awareness** – the other inter-related, inter-dependent bottom-up skill in the literacy process.

orthographic awareness
alertness to the spelling sequences that constitute written words

Developing orthographic awareness

The intricacies of the cognitive mechanisms that enable readers to recognise words instantaneously and automatically is debated by psychologists (as helpfully summarised and explained by Stuart, 1995 and Ehri, 1992). However, what is clear is that this facility develops over time and through many exposures to print and text. It is also incontrovertible from the research evidence that children process print in qualitatively different and increasingly complex ways en route both to becoming fluent in reading and being able to write coherent, accurate text.

For whole- or sight-words to be stored in an individual's **lexicon** (word memory bank or sight vocabulary), the words have to be 'learned' or seen so often that a **logogen** is formed. Each word has a logogen. The term has changed meaning with changing theories, but can be thought of as a kind of mental template against which perceptual instances of words are checked in order to permit identfication. This picture is created by the brain so that the entire image of the word can be *recalled* when writing or *recognised* when reading so that the meaning is accessed from the individual's memory store also.

lexicon
dictionary or, when used by psychologists, mental dictionary; refers to the memory store for words, their spellings and sounds

logogen
the mental construct employed by psychologists in discussing the ways words are represented in the mental **lexicon** to permit word recognition

This process is achieved through developmental stages and is influenced by the refinement of phonological awareness to a greater or lesser extent depending on your viewpoint or theoretical stance.

Several psychologists have suggested developmental stage theories of the print-processing abilities of early readers (Marsh, Friedman, Welch and Desberg, 1980; and Ehri, 1992). Frith's theory (1985) is discussed in this chapter because of its accessiblity and suitability for the declared purpose of this volume – it provides appropriate insight into the complexity of print-processing for those primary teachers who teach very young children to read.

Frith's phase theory

Frith's (1985) theory follows the following phases of sight-word reading:

- logographic phase
- alphabetic phase
- orthographic phase.

The logographic phase of sight-word reading

In the first stage of print-processing, as described by Frith (1985), the young child perceives words as wholes, or as logograms. The word is recognised by the child through personally memorable and highly distinctive visual features such as the typography in the typeface of the logo of Coca-Cola or Pepsi, the two 'dd's of 'Daddy', the 'sticks' in 'lollipop' or, as in 'Benjamin', the distinct shape/length and the two dots of 'i' and 'j'. The child has no recourse to phonological decoding as both the letters of the alphabet and the associated sounds are not known or salient to the reader at this very early stage of literacy development.

Children differ in the chronological age at which they pass through this stage. McGee, Lomax and Head (1988) conducted a study on pre-schoolers in the USA and stopped with the 5,000th 3-year-old as they all showed that they knew that the MacDonald's logo stands for hamburgers or MacDonald's. This indicates that with the context-rich support of the golden arch alongside the logo, children as young as 3 years old have no difficulty accessing the meaning of this symbol of contemporary culture. Without such support though, children are not always able to identify words in a traditional typeface, for example 'Coca-Cola' without the distinctive flowing red script. Similarly, emergent readers fail to notice the change from 'Pepsi' to 'Xepsi' if the typeface remains consistent with the distinctive logo.

Word identification is related to meaning (semantics) so heavily that phonetically regular words such as 'but' and 'dud' both so visually and semantically bland are virtually impossible to remember and spelling remains a mystery unless continually practised.

CASE STUDY

Attending to features of print

Some children remain arrested in this first stage of print-processing for some time after they go to school. For example, Peter in Stuart's (1995) study, when asked how he knew a word was 'television', replied 'Oh that's easy. It's got a dot. Actually it's got two dots, but anyway, I don't care' (p. 47). The implications for teaching children in this stage are important and will be addressed at the end of this section.

1 What does this mean that teachers have to do in order to know about their pupils' literacy development?
2 Why is it important for teachers to know how children are processing print?

The alphabetic phase of sight-word reading

The child moves into the next phase of print-processing as letters of the alphabet are learned by their distinguishing shape and names or sounds. Ehri (1992) maintains that it is this knowledge that provides the child with sufficient 'low-level phonemic awareness' that the beginnings and ends of words can be recognised and rudimentary sound–spelling connections can be made. Words are still remembered by their distinctive shape, and through the salience of the meaning, but a crude sound–symbol link is also attached to the recognition process for the word as it then is effectively committed to the lexical memory store, or sight vocabulary.

Many complex research studies (for example, Ehri and Wilce, 1985) have been undertaken with children in this stage of literacy development and here is the evidence of only one. It is clear that very soon after exposure to formal teaching, novice readers find nonsense words with a logical sound–symbol relationship easier to remember than words with arbitary letters used in them (for example, 'MSK' for 'mask' in the first case, and 'He' also representing 'mask' in the second case).

Early years teachers have the advantage of being able to analyse their pupils' writing to diagnose their print-processing ability accurately, providing, of course, that their pupils have been encouraged to use 'invented spelling' or 'emergent writing'. Children in the alphabetic phase of reading development typically display the semi-phonetic stage of writing described by Gentry (1981). For example, when in pupil's mark-making or writing there is evidence of some representation of letter–sound (grapheme–phoneme) correspondence, for example 'wnt' for 'went', 'hse' for 'house' and 'pse' for 'please' (See also page 101). These children are demonstrating that they are in the beginning stages of understanding the alphabetic principle – they are self-evidently getting to grips with the code. Not only is this crucial ability displayed conveniently for primary teachers *through* their mark-making or writing, but it is most powerfully developed into progressively more accurate phonemic segmentation and appropriate representation of the sound units by being explicitly *taught*. This is the most effective way of capitalising on the relationship between phonological and orthographic awareness to enable both abilities to develop side-by-side, complementing each other. The ability to recognise sight-words becomes more and more efficient through this stage of print-processing as the lexical memory store (word bank or sight vocabulary) enlarges.

The orthographic phase of sight-word reading

Ehri (1992) defines her equivalent of this phase of sight-word reading as:

the process of reading sight words by setting up connections in memory between the entire sequence of letters in spellings and phonemic constituents in the word's pronounciation.

That is, the reader is able to short-circuit the letter-by-letter phonological conversion of the previous stage through being able to process 'chunks' of print from sight memory. Frequently processed words and parts of words come to be retained in the lexical memory as recognition units that permit virtually automatic decoding and faster reading. Such chunking also helps with writing, through the encoding of spellings which thereby become more accurate.

Characteristically, digraphs (i.e. two letters representing one sound, for example, *ea* and *ee*; consonant digraphs, for example, *ch* , *sh* and *th*) and the phonemes that are represented are memorised and used appropriately. The 'silent e' or 'magic e' is distinguished and recognised as an exception. Phonemic segmentation is accurate as is a near perfect understanding of the English spelling system. Fluency is achieved as decoding becomes almost instantaneous.

A comparison between Frith's and Ehri's phase theories (see Figure 3.2) makes the earlier explanation more accessible. Ehri's terms for the phases are usefully descriptive of the processing available to the child in the different phases, but the terminology is very wordy for frequent reference in connected text.

Figure 3.2
Two models of reading development

Age	Frith (1985)	Ehri (1995)
3–5 years	Logographic phase	Pre-alphabetic phase
		Partial alphabetic phase
5–7 years	Alphabetic phase	Full alphabetic phase
7–9 years	Orthographic phase	Consolidated alphabetic phase

The comparison presents a simplified picture of Frith's and Ehri's phased models of reading development and how they relate to each other. Frith developed her model so that she could compare the literacy development of dyslexic children with 'normal' developmental patterns. She also included writing in her model, being interested in the way reading and writing developed slightly out of step but in interaction with each other. Ehri developed her model in relation to the contribution of alphabetic skills to the development and changing nature of sight-word recognition.

Although their terminologies and some of their interests and interpretations are different, their accounts are compatible. Both researchers start with recognising logographic/pre-alphabetic sight-word learning and show how, through developing alphabetic/graphic processes, letter-by-letter decoding is replaced by a more sophisticated form of sight-word recognition in which words are perceived in terms of known spelling patterns or chunks.

For both of them, the term 'phase' is perhaps preferable to 'stage' because progression is seen as cumulative and not clear-cut. Earlier modes of print-processing are retained, to be used when needed, in the learner's repertoire of reading strategies.

Large-scale studies and reading progress

Continuing evidence about the progress children make in becoming literate comes from the findings of the Infant School Study (Tizard *et al.*, 1988). This project followed a cohort of children in 33 inner-London schools from the end of the nursery class through to the end of infant school. The main aim was to investigate the progress of children in order to explain the reasons for their differing rates of attainment. Variables such as home background, ethnic origin and factors both within the school and *between* teachers are also explored, and their varying influences accounted for in the analyses of the data. At this level of complexity, it becomes a challenge in itself to explain the relationships between the different variables. The finding most relevant to this book is that of the positive relationship between a child being able to identify and label letters of the alphabet at the end of nursery and later progress in reading.

An important study of literacy development that followed 191 reception children through the first year of school has shed light on the way in which the child comes to grips with the complexity of the task of reading, and how teachers can have insight into the print-processing abilities of the new pupil (Riley, 1994, 1995a, 1996). This research project provides further evidence to support the value of the young reader's refined orthographic knowledge, indicated by the ability both to identify and label letters of the alphabet and to write her own name before formal instruction at school begins.

The most important finding is the relationship between the literacy-related skills assessed at school entry and reading (as measured by the raw score of the Neale's [1989] Analysis of Reading test) at the end of the first year of school.

The three literacy-related skills – concepts about print, ability to write her own name, and the ability to identify and label the letters of the alphabet – assessed by the researchers at school entry in September, were all shown to be positively related to the ability to read in the following July. However, the most powerful predictor, by far, of later success in reading was the child's knowledge of the alphabet. This was shown by the ability to identify and label the letters of the alphabet which had been acquired incidentally and informally pre-school.

This work adds considerable weight to the body of evidence that recognises that speedy word processing is essential for progress in reading, the first stage of which is an understanding of the alphabet system. A recognition of the individual letters, along with an ability to hear the sounds in words, are the first steps in the development of the orthographic and phonological processing capability essential in the literacy task.

The predictive value of the knowledge of the alphabet and the ability to write her own name is not a new finding: it re-affirms the views of Wells and Raban (1978) and the findings of the Infant School Study (Tizard *et al.*, 1988) regarding the strength of the association of orthographic knowledge and later reading. What is perhaps less appreciated is an explanation of these findings regarding the nature of the child's orthographic knowledge, which is shown by the continued influence of concepts about print in the statistical analyses.

Applying alphabetic knowledge

This finding suggests that it is not *knowing the alphabet* but *knowing how to apply* the knowledge of the alphabet that is important. In the next few paragraphs I will spell out the evidence for, and significance of, this claim.

The series of studies that followed the early finding, some 30 years ago, of the connection between knowledge of letters of the alphabet and early reading development (Chall, 1967; Bond and Dykstra, 1967) were disappointing. When Gibson and Levin (1975) and Ehri (1983) set out directly to teach children the letters of the alphabet, prior to school entry, there appeared to be no positive link with successful reading later.

Blatchford *et al.* (1987) suggest in their Infant School Study that the strong relationship found between letter knowledge on school entry and later reading probably reflects pre-school children's general acquaintance with written language.

I argue elsewhere (1994, 1995a) that the connection is more complex than that. The child who has shown that she can identify and label the letters of the alphabet probably comes to school with an understanding of the alphabetic code, and she is clearly further along on the path to reading.

Arriving at the levels of understanding that the child possesses about anything is not easy. The distinction between various levels of understanding of the alphabetic code is still more challenging. As the child moves from emergent literacy (see Chapter 4) to conventional reading, she develops through several levels of understanding from conceptual, to formal, through to symbolic understanding of letters. The symbolic relationship between letters and sounds is the basis of the English writing system, as discussed earlier. Vygotsky (1978) states:

> *A feature of this [writing] system is that it is second order symbolism, which gradually becomes direct symbolism. This means that written language consists of a system of signs that designate the sounds and words of spoken language, which, in turn are signs for real entities and relations.*

(Vygotsky, 1978, p. 106)

Bialystok (1991) conducted a study that explored this gradual shift in understanding of children between 3 and 5 years of age. She designed labelling and spelling tasks using plastic letters. Of all the assessment techniques, her 'moving word' task proved to be the most powerful predictor of success.

In this task, Bialystok used a 'naughty puppet' to move letters in words and it was the extent to which the children became concerned about this that she was able to ascertain the nature of their understanding of the alphabet. Through this, she concluded that the most essential insight is the symbolic relation by which letters represent sounds. This clearly needs to be capitalised upon in school with those children who show an early awareness of letter–sound correspondence and develop it into a gradual appreciation of the English alphabetic system and its complexities.

Bialystok writes:

> *Children's first achievement with letters is as part of a procedure, namely reciting the alphabet. . .Reading requires symbolic knowledge of letters. The representation must include the relation between the letter and its sound. Objects* have *meanings; symbols represent meanings. Objects can* make *sounds; Symbols* stand for *sounds. Meaning is somehow in* objects; *it is not in symbols. For this reason formal knowledge of the alphabet is not sufficient for learning to read.*

(Bialystok, 1991, p. 78)

This explains why the studies mentioned earlier, that set out merely to teach the alphabet by rote, had no enduring value and this fails to guarantee an early successful start to reading. The appreciation of the symbolic representation of letters for spoken sounds occurs slowly over time and with exposure to meaningful experiences of print and text.

In Bialystok's experimental group those children who could read were more successful in all the word tasks undertaken. They were the same age, and there was no significant difference between their levels of spoken language as demonstrated by receptive vocabulary scores, as the non-readers in the study. Bialystok suggests that:

> *the difference between those children who could read and those who could not has something to do with the way in which they understand the letter–sound correspondences.*

(Bialystok, 1991, p. 87)

Knowing letter names *or* sounds on entry to school indicates experience with print, cognitive and perceptual maturity and the requisite attention span, in addition to a symbolic understanding of the alphabet. The child's knowledge of spoken and written language offers access to the symbolic system. Downing (1979) provides a 'cognitive clarity' model which leads to a clearer and clearer appreciation of the alphabetic system. He asserts that superior letter-name knowledge is a symptom of a greater understanding of the technical features of writing and is one of the prerequisite concepts for fluent reading. Altogether they are:

- the concept that the continuous flow of speech can be segmented into parts
- the concept of the spoken word
- the concept of the phoneme
- the concept of code – that an abstract symbol can represent something else
- the concept of the written word
- the concept of the grapheme
- the concept of the letter.

Bialystok's study provides insight into different levels of ability to identify letters. These levels denote more advanced understandings of words and the symbolic nature of language. The child who has learned to identify her letters, incidentally as it were, over time, and through many meaningful encounters with print, has developed a deeper, more refined appreciation of the role of letters in the representation of sounds. The child who has this understanding at school entry is further along the road to reading than the child who is merely able to recite the alphabet. The level of the child's understanding and knowledge is of great importance to her teacher.

Adams (1993) hints at the transition phase of reading development when she writes:

> *For children who, on entering the classroom, do not yet have a comfortable familiarity with the letters of the alphabet, finding ways to help them is of first order importance. Even so, knowledge of letters is of little value unless the* child knows and is interested in their use. *Correctly perceived and interpreted, print conveys information. In keeping with this, children's concepts about print are also strong predictors of the ease with which they will learn to read. Before formal instruction is begun, children should possess a broad and general appreciation of the nature of print.*
>
> (Adams, 1993, p. 207)

IMPLICATIONS FOR PRACTICE

Working with the individual child in a supportive and diagnostic way

Nursery and reception class teachers need to be aware of the exact stage of literacy development of their young pupils. Concepts about print are acquired slowly through the emergent literacy phase; they develop through rich and meaningful encounters with print in the twin processes of early reading and primitive message writing. These crucial understandings are the prerequisite to the acquisition of conventional literacy and are discussed fully in Chapter 4. An integral aspect of this understanding is the child's gradual appreciation of the symbolic nature as distinct from the formal understanding of written language (Bialystok, 1991), of which the ability to identify and label non-sequential letters of the alphabet at school entry is an early indication. This is very different from the ability merely to recite the alphabet, as has been shown earlier.

Teachers working with young children need to be skilled, diagnostic facilitators of their early literacy attempts. At best, they mimic the parent or carer who before school so powerfully assisted valuable literacy progress. At worst, nursery and reception class teachers cut across the child's rich but highly personal prior learning to confuse and dishearten (Baker and Raban, 1991) (see Chapter 4 for further discussion).

Clay promotes careful, recorded observation of reading behaviours in the very early stages of literacy in order to inform the next step in teaching:

> *Sensitive and systematic observation of behaviour is really the only way to monitor gradual shifts across imperfect responding.*
>
> (Clay, 1991, p. 233)

She goes on to list her signs of a developing inner control in the areas of:

- using language (both spoken and 'mark-making' written language)
- gaining concepts about print
- attending to visual information
- hearing sounds in sequence.

The beginning reader gradually learns how to integrate the processes and the teacher needs to monitor and analyse the progress systematically. Clay displays clearly the monitoring of the child's reading strategies that need to be assessed by the teacher (see Figure 3.3).

Figure 3.3
Sources of information about text

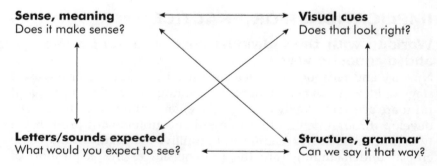

(Clay and Cazden, 1990, reprinted in Moll, 1990, p. 207)

Teaching follows the sensitive observation. The first assessment will occur on entry to school and is covered in Chapter 4. All aspects of the child's reading can be supported with great benefit, through sharply focused teaching appropriate for the developmental stage and level of competence the child has in using the various strategies.

Realistically, it is recognised that children will not be taught as individuals. However, it is important for teachers to be aware of the learning needs of *each* child in order to provide learning experiences that will enable reading to develop.

National Curriculum (Pre-Level 1)

Observation of the child reading

The following list covers some of the literacy behaviours that are characteristically displayed by the child at this stage of development.

- *Literacy behaviour* is displayed by the child by:
  - enjoying books
  - attempting to read known text (acting like a reader)
  - concentrating on the literacy activity in hand.

- *Understanding of the literacy task* is shown by:
  - knowing that print has a communicative function
  - being aware of environmental print, i.e. recognises labels, notices, messages
  - knowing the conventions of print, i.e. can point to where you start reading, knows sweep back on line, knows where to go to on the following page.

Teaching approaches to support print and sound awareness

Children at this stage are in the emergent literacy phase of development (see Chapter 4). They will be able to recognise a few highly distinctive, personally relevant words as logograms (i.e. as whole words).

- *Sound awareness* (phonological awareness) can be encouraged by:
  - attention being drawn to sounds in words (bilingual learners should be encouraged to do this both in their home language and English) to develop phonological awareness, for example, 'All those people who have a name beginning with P go and sit in their places', playing games, for example, taking out of a 'magic' bag a selection of items all beginning with the same initial sound
  - listening to and reciting poems, rhymes, jingles, songs and nursery rhymes
  - explicit teaching of rhyme through learning of the written (class) rhyme of the week (using a commercially-published chart or written on a large piece of card), working from books with rhyming text, brainstorming additional rhyming words on a flip chart
  - introducing letter–sound correspondences through alphabet identification and learning (use of commercial materials, for example Letterland, can be helpful) to recognise, learn and name letters. Also this can be done very effectively through handwriting practice with a scheme such as Jolly Phonics
  - having book bins of multiples of high-quality alphabet picture books (for example, by Brian Wildsmith, or Shirley Hughes) for children to browse through
  - alphabet friezes round the room (at the appropriate height) and also fixed (with plastic seal) to the pupils' tables or Oxford Reading Tree alphabet mats for use on the work table of the individual child
  - containers of plastic letters (upper and lower case) for constant use in relation to grapheme–phoneme (letter–sound) association work, this is especially valuable when the child is writing at this stage of development

- use of games such as deleting initial phonemes or onset of a word, for example, *c*-ar, *P*-at, *d*-og.
- *Print awareness* (orthographic awareness) can be encouraged by drawing attention to:
  - distinctive words in familiar texts, for example, the names of characters in books
  - familiar words in environmental print, for example, labels and notices
  - children's names in the class
  - opportunities for mark-making and 'invented spelling' both with adults and independently, for example, making cards, writing letters and notes, labels and notices, provide literacy activities in the home corner and adaptations of it, for example, a MacDonald's, a hospital, a bakery
  - class-made books with familiar, repetitive text from combinations of photos of the children incorporating their names in the text or familiar logos, for example:

    For breakfast Jane likes *Cornflakes*

    Ahmed likes *Shreddies*

National Curriculum Level 1 (Early Stage)

Observation of the child reading
The following literacy behaviours that denote progress are characteristically displayed by the child at this stage of literacy development.

- *Literacy behaviour* is displayed by:
  - reading known text with much adult support
  - pointing word-by-word as she/he or adult reads, i.e. approximate one-to-one correspondence of written to spoken word; stabbing with finger at known words and sliding over unknown words
  - will substitute unknown words with no graphic accuracy but with sense in the context (for example, house for flat).
- *Understanding of the literacy task* is shown by:
  - being able to discuss books and plot at literal level
  - beginning to appreciate that long words when spoken will require a correspondingly long symbol when written, i.e. noticing that it must be 'bicycle' not 'bike'.
- *Print-processing skills* of the child are demonstrated by:
  - accurate knowledge of the alphabet
  - ability to recognise a few high-frequency words out of context
  - being able to point to a letter in a word (this skill often starts with letters in the child's name)

- being able to read back own caption under a painting
- having, towards the end of this phase, acquired a small sight vocabulary linked to her interests, the reading scheme and National Literacy Strategy *Framework for Teaching* high-frequency words.

Teaching approaches at NC Level 1 (Early Stage)

Children at this stage are moving from the emergent literacy phase towards the beginning of conventional reading. They have a sight vocabulary of a few words that they recognise as logograms. They need now to be supported into the alphabetic phase.

- *Sound awareness* (phonological awareness) can be supported by:
  - encouraging recognition of and ability to write each letter of the alphabet by emphasising the letter shape and its correct formation and its sound, Jolly Phonics are helpful for this (always teach letters in handwriting sessions in shape families, for example, c, a, g, d)
  - using a flip chart to reinforce the above for whole-class hand-writing
  - helping awareness of grapheme–phoneme (letter–sound) association through initial sound work, starting with children's names
  - free writing for a range of purposes and the child is encouraged to use 'invented spelling' in order to represent the sounds in words with a symbol. With adult support (most likely in a small-group situation), the segmentation (separation) of sounds in words can be reinforced and linked to the alphabet friezes on wall and on the table or with plastic letters. This is a very important activity and should be carried out very frequently at this stage of reading. The adult provides feedback (i.e. making things explicit) on what the child understands about the alphabetic system
  - work in groups on awareness of onset and rime, both aurally and visually.
- *Print awareness* (orthographic awareness, now word recognition) is supported by helping children to:
  - make their own books with repetitive texts using photos, names or familiar words to represent their on-going interests
  - recognise their own name from a list of names
  - write their own name correctly with an emphasis on both letter formation and the constituent letters
  - identify and read high-frequency words through writing and games located in a meaningful context

- recognise that its length and shape is a cue for identifying a word (i.e. what the word *looks* like)
- play games matching word card to pictures, for example, photos to children's names, name cards to characters in reading schemes, etc.

National Curriculum Level 1 (Later Stage)

Observation of the child reading

Literacy behaviours that denote progress characteristically displayed by the child at this stage of literacy development are given below.

- *Progress in reading* is displayed by:
  - slowing down when reading as the child works hard at processing the text
  - starting to show awareness of mismatch by self-correcting, plus evidence of scanning ahead
  - spelling is becoming more conventional when writing, using 'invented spelling' on her own text.
- *Understanding of the literacy task* is demonstrated by:
  - being able to use all the four cueing systems – *context* (including picture cue), *syntax* and the *look of the word*, i.e. length/distinctive features, *phonic analysis* (see Figure 3.3). The use of the strategies will be erratic with over-reliance on first one then another cue, but nevertheless the awareness of the different aspects of decoding print is developing
  - beginning to consider the plot and character of the story in greater detail.
- *Print-processing skills* of the child are demonstrated by having an increasing sight-word vocabulary (approximately 50 words).

Teaching approaches at NC Level 1 (Later Stage)

Use activities as appropriate for the earlier stages. The child will have moved from the logographic through to the alphabetic phase of print processing and will have both strategies at her disposal for reading and writing.

- *Sound awareness* (phonological awareness) is supported by:
  - making explicit the grapheme–phoneme (letter–sound) correspondence when reading and writing
  - listening to dominant phonemes (including consonant digraphs *ch*, *sh*)
  - blending phonetically regular two/three-letter words (consonant/vowel/consonant – CVC), for example, m/a/n (including nonsense words w/u/g)

- identifying words that rhyme with familiar sight vocabulary, for example, can. . .fan, tan, pan, ran
- using knowledge of initial sounds to act as a cue to make a choice between two or three words within the sight vocabulary when reading connected text
- using analogy to help write new words from known ones, for example, *t-ook* from *b-ook.*
- *Print awareness* (orthographic awareness/word recognition) is developed by:
  - practising sight vocabulary with games, context sentence cards (both commercial and teacher-made), with and without pictures, or whole stories
  - using correct spellings of a few common words in the course of her own writing. Attention can be drawn to the standard spelling (of one or two words only) with word lists in the classroom or personal word banks when appropriate and in context.

Additional teaching note:
Handwriting practice develops formation of letter shapes and also reinforces grapheme–phoneme correspondence. Also note that it is at this stage that print and sound awareness become more strongly linked and mutually reinforcing.

National Curriculum Level 2
The following is a list of literacy behaviours that denote progress characteristically displayed at this stage of literacy development.

Observation of the child reading

- *Progress in literacy* is displayed by:
  - being able to read known text independently
  - beginning to attempt unknown text, well motivated to try.
- *Understanding of the literacy task* is demonstrated by:
  - reading more fluently
  - being more able to integrate cueing strategies when decoding an unknown word
  - being able to discuss stories with insight of character and plot.
- *Print-processing skills* are demonstrated by having a sight vocabulary of approximately 100 words.
  Children will now be moving to the orthographic stage of processing text from the alphabetic stage, i.e. they are able to recognise groups of letters by their spelling patterns and without letter-by-letter conversion. At times readers still use processing abilities of earlier stages (logographic and alphabetic).

- *Sound awareness* (phonological awareness) is supported by helping children to perfect understanding of grapheme–phoneme association in both their reading and writing using 'invented spelling' and the use of:
  - rhyming words
  - consonant digraphs and blends
  - phonograms (onset and rimes)
  - synthesis of words into syllables.
- *Print awareness* (orthographic awareness/word recognition) is supported by:
  - learning sight-word vocabulary in both text, games and environmental print
  - helping children to spell known words in the course of their own writing by drawing attention to use of word banks, key word lists, etc.
  - encouraging familiarity with letter strings and patterns in words (this can be done during handwriting practice also)
  - drawing attention to words with common prefixes and suffixes
  - helping the decoding of unknown words by analogy with a known word, for example, shook/look.

Additional teaching note:
Handwriting is taught concurrently with the above, but not when the child is writing freely and using invented spelling and when composition is the focus.

(The implications for practice were developed from Riley, 1996.)

Summary

The similarities and differences between learning to speak and learning to read and write have been discussed. The main focus of this chapter has been on the decoding skills of reading, known as bottom-up processing. For the young child to become a fluent, accurate and fast reader, she has to be able to break words into their constituent sounds (i.e. to segment phonemes) and to map those sounds onto the relevant letters or groups of letters accurately. This aspect of literacy requires an understanding of the alphabetic code which takes several years to achieve through exposure to print and text, as well as focused, direct teaching.

The key points that have been addressed in this chapter are:

- **the development of phonological awareness**
- **the development of orthographic awareness**

● **how to support these aspects of reading in the early years classroom.**

Riley, J.L. (1996) *The Teaching of Reading: The Development of Literacy in the Early Years of School,* London: Paul Chapman Publishing
This book describes the research project mentioned in this chapter that investigated the literacy development of pupils during the first year of school.

Funnell, E. and Stuart, M. (eds) (1995) *Learning to Read: Psychology in the Classroom,* Oxford: Blackwell
This book is based on psychological research (much of it carried out by the authors) and explains in greater detail the development of print and sound awareness.

Further reading

4 Emergent literacy

Objectives   *When you have read this chapter, you should:*

- understand how the young pre-school child gradually becomes aware of the purpose and conventions of print and text

- appreciate that different children have had a variety of opportunities and a range of experiences with written language before coming to school

- know how important it is for the reception teacher to be aware of each pupil's stage of literacy development in order to be able to support progress well.

Introduction

There has been great interest in recent years in children as cognitive beings, children who selectively attend to aspects of their environments seeing, searching, remembering, monitoring, correcting, validating and problem-solving – activities which build cognitive competencies. . .Because of what we now know about oral language acquisition we have to accept that children can be active constructors of their own language competencies. Too often we adopt teaching strategies which proceed as if this were not true.

(Clay, 1991, p. 61)

The first section of this volume (Chapters 1 to 3) considers in depth how the young child learns that spoken language is about communicating meaning and then realises, over time and through experiences with print, that written language is the permanent equivalent of speech. The child learns how to make literacy her own re-invention, in similar ways that she previously learned to do with spoken language. Through literacy she is able to reconstruct the world for herself. First, a fundamental and global understanding occurs at a conceptual level or 'the big picture' (Purcell-Gates, 1996) about the purpose of written language. This precedes the finer-grained and multi-layered insights regarding conventions of print. Later still, the reader comes to appreciate the nature and function of the symbols in an alphabetic system. These complex strands have to be unravelled gradually, in personally purposeful situations, and in sympathy with Vygotsky's belief that 'Literacy is not a unitary construct' (1978).

EMERGENT LITERACY – NOT PRE-READING

This notion of a slow initiation into text and print has led to the use of the term 'emergent literacy'. It was devised by Marie Clay in 1966 and has replaced an earlier belief in a state of 'pre-reading' and is the term used to describe 'the reading and writing behaviours that precede and develop into conventional literacy' (Sulzby, 1989, p. 728). Emergent literacy describes the journey from a very primitive starting point 'looking at and responding to' nursery images in a cardboard booklet in the 'Baby's First Picture Book' category. This understanding is followed by the recognition of recurring signs in environmental print, such as a supermarket logo (seen both on the building and on the carrier bag) and then the awareness of alphabet symbols as repeated shapes in names, in books, on a frieze, on greetings cards, on the TV, and when playing games and puzzles and finally through to fully fluent reading of whole text in story books. A wealth of research evidence, undertaken mainly through an ethnographic methodology (i.e. data collected mainly by in-depth observation and case studies), has informed researchers and primary teachers of the many idiosyncratic twists and turns on this journey.

A great deal is now known about the child's competence as she begins to understand:

- the links between speech and writing
- the unchanging nature of print
- its communicative function and its conventions.

Importantly, in direct consequence of these research findings through the 1980s, development in reading and writing began increasingly to be viewed as the complementary processes of literacy. This work has far-reaching implications for practice in early years classrooms.

How do pre-school children come to acquire these understandings?

As Goodman (1980) claims, the 'roots of literacy' awareness develop through living in a world of story books, letters, lists and printed materials, and are the beginning of the child's fascination with print. The prime understanding of the young child, acquired gradually from 6 months to approximately 5 or 6 years of age, is that print has a communicative function (Ferreiro and Teberosky, 1982; Goodman, 1980). The child grows to understand the purpose of print in a personal and context-embedded way: typically through birthday cards, MacDonald's signs and biscuit packets (McGee, Lomax and Head, 1988, cited by Sulzby and Teale, 1991).

The sharing of story and picture books has received the most attention from researchers, not surprisingly, as it is the child's main and most sustained literacy experience prior to mainstream school and the formal task of learning to read. The benefits of reading stories as a socially created, interactive activity (Heath, 1982) are now clear. The young child's independent but as yet not conventional reading of books grows out of shared interactive reading with a facilitative adult and provides a scaffold to her literacy development (Sulzby, 1989). Wells (1988) found a strong positive relationship between the number of stories shared with pre-school children and their later success in reading throughout the primary and secondary school.

Two important features of this work

There are two features that result from this body of work on the emergent literacy phase observation that have the most relevance to early years teachers.

- Firstly, the research findings view the child as an active contributor to her own learning. The meaning-maker of spoken language is at work here also. This learner-centred view of the pre-school reader and writer is greatly influenced by Piaget, Bruner and Chomsky, each of whom see the child as being a constructive, hypothesis-testing, rule-generating agent in her own learning. This view has been emphasised extensively in Chapters 1 and 2.
- Secondly, the studies cited highlight the role of the supportive, interested, interactive and experienced language user, who scaffolds the child's learning in order that progress can occur.

These two crucial aspects of literacy learning have implications for the later phases of development as a reader and a writer. The child has mastered an important lesson about how to learn both about and through spoken and written language. Teachers need not only to note the ways that such valuable learning has occurred, but also to appreciate *what* has been learned in order to build appropriately on these highly individual foundations.

What the child has learned about literacy before school

If we begin from the point of entry to school, it appears that the most common and essential lessons about literacy that the young child can achieve before school are that:

- reading is a pleasurable and useful activity
- print has a communicative function
- written scripts have a set of rules and conventions that need to be adhered to
- text has a meta-language which the child needs to become acquainted with – the set of terms used to describe aspects and functions of print, for example, 'letter', 'word', 'sentence', 'beginning', 'end', 'full stop', 'comma'.

The research literature into emergent literacy indicates that there are three main types of experience which lead to the print-related achievements to which reference has been made. They are:

- home literacy experience
- story book experience
- teaching by parents.

HOME LITERACY EXPERIENCE

Young children have the most fruitful opportunities to develop their understandings of literacy within the home environment. The learners are able to practise the language systems, both spoken and written, through interactions with others in a personal, secure and a very specific cultural context. Gee (1992) refers to this as the **situated dialogue** of the **cultural practice** in the home community. By this it is meant that children begin to learn about reading and writing in their homes and within their communities through observing and participating in culturally-situated literacy practices (Ferreiro and Teberosky, 1982). This seminal work has been built upon and refined by Purcell-Gates (1996) to clarify the nature of the different emphases placed by various communities on particular literacy practices. It is recognised that literacy practices differ between communities in a variety of socio-cultural dimensions and it is known that the child's pre-school and deeply personal experience profoundly influences success at school (Dyson, 1989; Riley, 1995a and 1995b).

Recent research studies into pre-school home literacy experiences

Concern about the wide range in the levels of school-orientated success experienced by various socio-economic groups has fuelled recent research projects. Several studies from the USA have documented that whilst literacy is integral to the lives of both high and lower socio-economic groups, the experiences and therefore what the children make of them differ. As a group, children from lower socio-economic groups tend to achieve lower levels of literacy skill

situated dialogue
dialogue that is embedded and given meaning by its context in a shared situation, e.g. 'Don't!'; more widely, dialogue embedded in lifestyle and value systems

cultural practice
value-embued activities and situations characteristic of a cultural or subcultural lifestyle, e.g., the birthday party, the stag night, the dinner party, the bed-time story

once at school than the children from higher income groups. It has been assumed by the research community that one of the most salient factors causing this differential in success is that the different levels of education of the parents affects the nature and complexity of the literacy activities at home to which the children are party.

Teale remarked that the findings 'should prompt a reconsideration of traditional wisdom which has it that children from low-Socio-economic status (SES) backgrounds come to school with a dearth of literacy experiences' (1986, p. 192). Taylor and Dorsey-Gaines (1988) conducted an ethnographic study into the lives of five low-SES families whose children were successful in school. These children were observed participating in story and Bible reading events, they saw their parents reading newspapers, magazines and writing to various social service agencies and to schools.

Investigations of the types of literacy experienced by the child

Further studies have attempted to separate out the dimensions of the home literacy environment and to quantify the ways in which they influence the child's knowledge about written language. The three identified dimensions of literacy experiences participated in by children in their home environments were:

- interacting with adults in writing and reading situations
- exploring print on their own
- observing adults modelling literate behaviours (for example, reading instructions/writing lists).

data-narrative
diary, coding and recording behaviours of subjects

After many hours of detailed observation in the homes of lower-SES families completing a **data narrative**, or description, the presence of varied literacy activities were indeed confirmed by the Purcell-Gates (1996) study. The types of literacy event that the children were likely to participate in or to witness were systematically coded. These categories covered aspects such as literacy connected with the following:

- *daily living routines*, for example, shopping, cooking, paying bills, etc.
- *entertainment*, for example, reading a novel, doing a crossword, reading a TV programme guide, reading rules for a game
- *school-related activity*, for example, letters from school to home, homework, playing school
- *work*, for example, literacy used in order to secure or maintain a job
- *religion*, for example, Bible reading or study, Sunday School activities
- *interpersonal communication*, for example, sending cards, writing and reading letters
- *story reading*.

In addition, the texts used by the adults were analysed for the linguistic complexity at vocabulary, sentence and clause levels.

Purcell-Gates found that there was considerable variation in the quality of the print experiences to which the children were exposed. This she attributed to different levels of the **functional literacy** present in the 20 families studied and this was clearly related, as was suggested earlier, to the educational level of the adults.

functional literacy
the level of literacy needed to operate reasonably effectively in a literate society

The literacy levels ranged from low literate (n = 3) to functionally literate (n = 17). These levels were estimated in the study through the application of a broad definition of functional literacy as being the:

> *possession of, or access to, the competencies and information required to accomplish transactions entailing reading and writing [in] which an individual wishes or is compelled to engage.*

> (Kintgen, Kroll and Rose, 1988, p. 263)

Then the study, using an innovative methodology, linked the home literacy experiences of the child to her knowledge of written language, in an attempt to unravel the connections between pre-school experience and success with literacy at school. In these lower-SES families, the most frequently observed print event was literacy being used in the domains of *entertainment* and *daily living routines*. These rich data make compulsive reading, as the fabric of the families and their daily existence emerges from the journal pages. Purcell-Gates says:

> *Pre-schoolers whose home lives included more instances of people reading and writing texts at the more written level of discourse demonstrated more conventional concepts of writing as a system and Concepts about Print. They also showed a higher degree of knowledge of written register the more their parents read to them. Children's story book text was considered the most complex text for this study. Kindergarten and first grade children who experienced people in their home and community lives reading and writing at the most written level of discourse also demonstrated a more advanced understanding of writing as a system.*

> (Purcell-Gates, 1996, p. 423)

It would seem that homes at all levels of socio-economic status and education offer many and varied opportunities for children to develop understanding about spoken and written language. What appears to differ is the *quality* of the encounters and the extent to which they are capitalised upon by the adults. It is not productive, therefore, for primary teachers to make professional judgements about the ways in which pupils will approach the task of literacy once at school, on the basis of socio-economic status and the educational level of parents. Much depends upon the child's **transactional stance** to learning – her ability to make sense of the learning opportunities offered by school and the extent to which it builds on the home experience. This, in turn, is affected by the teacher's ability to assess the child's prior knowledge at school entry and so to be able to provide well-matched learning activities. This issue will be developed further later in this chapter.

transactional stance
attitude and approach,
preparedness and
receptivity

Story book reading and parent teaching

A Canadian study (Senechal, Lefevre, Thomas and Daley, 1998) attempted both to quantify and to differentiate between the particular contributions that the reading of stories and the direct teaching of pre-school children make to the level of success at school with oral and written language skills. This is currently a much debated arena of research into emergent literacy in North America. It reduces down to the relative importance of the young child's understanding of 'the big picture' about literacy and her grasp of the alphabetic principle. This, in turn, is a late 1990s and focused version of the whole language versus phonics debate that has raged, in a counterproductive manner, through at least two previous decades of literacy research on both sides of the Atlantic. Also, on a note of caution, much depends, as always, on the research design for such studies. The results are dependent upon the nature of the outcomes to be measured, both at the conceptual level of the outcomes being investigated *and* the assessments used to measure the outcomes. However, these studies do have important implications for early years teachers.

In summary, the findings from this study (Senechal *et al.*, 1998) and other studies are that:

> *parents distinguish between two different kinds of experiences with print at home. Some experiences provide more informal or implicit interactions with print such as when parents read to the child. In this kind of experience, children are exposed to written language, but print* per se *is not the focus of interactions. Other experiences provide more formal or explicit interactions with print such as when parents teach about reading and writing words and letters.*

(Senechal *et al.*, 1998, p. 109)

The distinction between the informal and the formal, it would seem, is whether the focus of the experience offered the child is on the message contained *in the print* or *about the print itself*. The analyses of the data from the Senechal *et al.* (1998) study indicate that the different kinds of literacy experiences are related to the development of different kinds of literacy-related skills. More research needs to be done with greater numbers of children at all levels of socio-economic status, but at a basic level this work is revealing to teachers that children learn from the experiences they are exposed to and what they are taught. Educationalists need to be clear about what is important in order to advise parents appropriately.

It would seem wise to suggest that young children are given broad, balanced and meaningful experiences with written language so that they can be successful at school. They need, as stated earlier, to become aware of the purpose of print and its rules and conventions. This level of understanding at entry to school prepares the way for beginning of conventional reading.

THE BEGINNING OF CONVENTIONAL READING

The point at which the reader moves from emergent literacy into beginning conventional reading is not clear. Sulzby (1992) defines this transition point as being when the child is able to use the following three aspects of reading in a flexible and co-ordinated way:

- letter–sound knowledge
- the concept of a word
- comprehension.

Sulzby states that the transition point is blurred as the child's imperfect understanding regresses and advances through many print encounters, before finally moving into conventional print processing.

For a detailed explanation of the developmental path of fluent reading, it is necessary to draw upon experimental psychology to shed light on the young child's print-processing abilities as she enters the phase of beginning reading. These have been described by several researchers as phases or stages during which the child processes the print in *qualitatively* different ways. Frith (1985) and Ehri (1995) propose a phase theory of progressively more refined print-processing abilities of the beginner reader. These theories have been compared and discussed fully in Chapter 3.

The nature of the knowledge of the alphabet and its importance

A study of literacy development, that followed 191 reception children through the first year of school, has shed light on the way in which the child gets to grips with the complexity of the task of reading, and how teachers can have insight into the print-processing abilities of the new pupil (Riley, 1994, 1995a, 1996). This research project, discussed in Chapter 3, provides further important evidence to indicate the value of the young reader's refined print awareness, shown in the ability both to identify and label letters of the alphabet and to write her own name before formal instruction begins at school.

The three literacy-related skills – concepts about print, the ability to write her own name, and the ability to identify and label the letters of the alphabet – assessed by the researchers in the September, were all shown to be positively related to the ability to read in the following July. But by far the most powerful predictor of later success in reading was the child's knowledge of the alphabet, acquired pre-school incidentally and informally.

This work adds considerable weight to the body of evidence that recognises that speedy word processing is essential for progress in reading, the first stage of which is an understanding of the alphabet system. A recognition of the individual letters, along with an ability to hear the sounds in words, are the first steps in the development of the orthographic (print) and phonological (sound) processing capability essential in the literacy task.

The importance of capitalising on what children know at school entry

We have discussed how children come to school with different levels of literacy knowledge acquired through a variety of experiences in their homes and communities. It is argued, therefore, that teachers need to be aware of those understandings. But why exactly is it important for reception teachers to harness this hard won pre-school knowledge as quickly and effectively as possible?

The most striking reason is that there is robust longitudinal evidence on the long-term benefits of an effective early start to mainsteam school. The earliest study to point to the first year of school as being of special importance is American and 20 years old (Pedersen, Faucher and Eaton, 1978). These researchers found that a group of children who had been taught by a particular first grade teacher, 'Miss A', seemed to have been given an initial boost to their education that gave an advantage throughout the remainder of their schooling. The research methodology was unusual and retrospective. The researchers used the school annual report cards to track the academic progress of the groups of children in 'Miss A's' school (i.e. the annual scores over many years, of all the classes from entry in elementary through to exit from secondary school). It seemed that this exceptional teacher achieved results with her pupils in early literacy and numeracy far beyond those of her colleagues with parallel and comparable intakes.

Large-scale longitudinal studies
More recent evidence comes from the findings of the Infant School Study (Tizard *et al.*, 1988). This interesting project followed a cohort of children in 33 inner-London schools from the end of nursery through to the end of infant school. The main aim was to investigate the progress of children in order to explain the reasons for their differing rates of educational achievement. The most important finding is that it was only in the reception year that certain classes made statistically significant greater rates of progress than others. Also, the project showed that those children who had made the greatest amount of progress in reception remained the highest achievers all through infant school.

As Tizard says, 'We had evidence that the reception year has a particularly large effect on progress'. Tizard *et al.* followed-up part of the sample of children at the end of primary school (at 11 years old) and the rank order of the children's scores had not changed. So, over seven years of primary school an early positive start appears to be important.

Another influential study, the Junior School Project (Mortimore *et al.*, 1988) confirms this research finding. This parallel project explored the organisation and the teaching and learning processes of the years 7–11 or Years 3, 4, 5 and 6. Amongst many other important findings, Mortimore *et al.* found that the rank order of children's test scores remained constant over the four years. In other words, how well the children were doing at the start of junior school predicted powerfully how well they would be doing at 11 years of age. This once again confirms the benefit of a successful, early start to school. These children were followed up to the end of secondary school (Sammons *et al.*, 1994). The pupils who had been the highest achievers at the end of primary school were those who gained the best GCSE results. We know, from the large body of research into school effectiveness, that school *does* make a difference to children's academic progress. It is suggested also that a positive start is especially important if an educational career is to be successful. Learning to read early and accurately will be a crucial part of that valuable beginning.

Studies focusing on the reception year
An explanation of why it is the first year that is quite so important has begun to emerge. Two studies exploring the teaching–learning

processes in the reception year of school have complemented each other in an interesting way that adds to our understanding. Aubrey (1993) and Riley (1994) point to the fact that the new pupil brings a rich store of knowledge and skills to the task of learning mathematics (Aubrey) and acquiring literacy (Riley, 1995a) in school. Children have learned a great deal through their experience of living in a world operating with a number rule system and surrounding them with print. Both these studies show that the challenge to the reception teacher is to diagnose 'where the child is' in her/his understanding in order to facilitate progress.

The two studies complement the findings of each other well. As Aubrey writes:

> *Whilst they may not possess the formal conventions for representing it, reception age children clearly enter school having acquired already much mathematical content.*

(Aubrey, 1993)

I found great disparity in literacy development: some children were functioning, at school entry, at the level of a 3-year-old with only the haziest understanding of how books and print work, whilst other pupils were well on the road to beginning reading. Some of the teachers were aware of the differences in their new entrants and sought to design reading programmes that matched the development precisely. Other reception class teachers used a 'scatter gun' approach and randomly tried a variety of methods in the hope that 'something must work'.

The pupils who made the most progress during their first year of school were taught by experienced reception class teachers who were knowledgeable about literacy and able to match closely their teaching to the child's prior and developing competence (Riley, 1996). Aubrey had similar findings in her study regarding the children's progress in mathematics.

IMPLICATIONS FOR PRACTICE

Fisher (1992) says:

> *children starting school are already successful and active learners who bring considerable knowledge and experience to the task of literacy learning. Children learn best when they are able to relate what they are doing to their own experience. They also learn most successfully when the learning takes place within a social context, particularly from interaction with a caring adult or more experienced child.*

Home is a good place to learn and, although homes vary, there is
much to be learned from the way the child has learned in the home.

(Fisher, 1992, p. 36)

The essential role of assessment at school entry

As earlier discussion has revealed, early years educators working
with young children need to be both skilled teachers and have the
ability to diagnose their pupils' early literacy learning. At best they
mimic the role of the adult who has facilitated so much valuable
literacy progress before school.

The information gathered at school entry for baseline assessment
enables meaningful comparison to be made with attainment, as
measured by the National Curriculum Tasks and Tests, at the end
of Key Stage 1. Increasing accountability is required from schools
and evidence of effective teaching is sought by inspectors and
governing bodies.

However, the main purpose of assessing the pupil on arrival at
school is to provide insight into the child's abilities and understandings in order to inform teaching usefully.

Information that the class teacher needs to record

General information on the child

Some of this information will be noted at school entry and up-dated
as appropriate and with any progress recorded also. It is suggested
that the following details are kept on individual children if they
are not included in the current LEA baseline assessment data expectations:

- relevant admission data, including number of siblings, child's
  place in family, etc. (it is especially important, for bilingual children whose parents are not fluent English speakers, that the
  school knows if there are older English-speaking siblings who can
  help with literacy)
- pre-school experience regarding length of attendance at nursery
  or playgroup
- relevant information about attitudes, concerns and expectations
  of parents or carers resulting from discussion with them
- relevant medical information regarding hearing, sight and general
  health
- level of general physical and social development
- evidence of the level of the child's self-esteem and confidence
- ability to care for herself regarding dressing, toileting, etc.
- evidence of child's level of adjustment to the class/school setting,
  including her ability to integrate with her peers.

Aspects of the child's intellectual functioning

Aspects of the child's intellectual functioning that need to be recorded are:

- relevant information gathered from observing the child at play in structured and unstructured activities
- the child's ability to concentrate on a task for periods of time
- the child's ability to represent the world and herself (for example, draw herself)
- the colours known
- the numbers known (are letters and numbers confused?)
- the nursery rhymes known.

Assessment of the child's spoken language

The teacher needs to assess the child's spoken language, as follows:

- whether English is the first or additional language (if English is the additional language: the details of the home language/s; whether the home language is spoken at home solely or in addition to English; the level of the English fluency of parents/carers)
- the level of confidence when communicating with adults or peers
- the ability to respond to questions, directions and requests
- the ability to communicate needs, ideas and feelings
- the ability to listen to stories and explanations.

Assessment of the child's understanding of written language

The teacher needs to make an assessment of the child's understanding of written language, its purpose and conventions, as follows.

- *Concepts about print*
  - Does the child demonstrate an awareness that signs and labels communicate a message (i.e. show awareness of pupils' name labels, labels on boxes and equipment, signs in the home corner, etc.)
  - When sharing a book does the child indicate understanding:
    that the story starts at the front of the book
    of the terms front and back
    that the print tells the story
    where the print starts, and which way it goes
    the convention of the 'sweep back' (i.e. the place of the next word at the end of a line)
    of the meta-language of print – word, letter, sentence, full-stop
    that within a word there are individual letters.
- *Print awareness* is demonstrated by:
  - the number of letters (by either name or sound, upper or lower case) of the alphabet that can be recognised and identified

- the ability to use some written marks in order to express herself and to communicate.
- *Sound awareness* is demonstrated by the ability to:
  - hear *very* distinctly different words, i.e. *sat/chat/fat/Jane*
  - detect words that rhyme from non-rhyming words, for example, m-*at*/h-*at*/c-*at*/r-*ap*
  - detect words with the same onset, for example, *m*-an/*m*-at/ *m*-ap/c-an.
- *Positive attitudes to books and literacy* are demonstrated by:
  - voluntarily looking at books with enjoyment
  - writing notes, messages and stories spontaneously
  - enjoy hearing stories read
  - valuing and caring for books.

(The above information was developed from Riley, 1996.)

This list conveys suggestions of observations of the reception child to be carried out and recorded by the class teacher. Levels of functioning on arrival at school (or at a pre-decided time soon after arrival) provide evidence of the child's specific needs regarding the provision for literacy teaching. In addition, these assessments enable the reception teacher to provide appropriate experiences and opportunities within her class and to inform her organisation and grouping of the pupils.

Summary

This chapter has considered the understandings about literacy that are acquired by the pre-school child and their importance for learning to read and write once at school. Research evidence suggests that not only are great strides made by the child in the emergent literacy phase, but also that this knowledge contributes hugely towards success once at school. The importance of the role of the teacher in assessing this informal and personal knowledge, so that it can be capitalised upon, has been discussed.

The key points that have been addressed in this chapter are that:

- **there is an emergent literacy phase of development**

- **it is necessary to assess the child's knowledge of literacy at school entry.**

Further reading

Riley, J.L. (1996) *The Teaching of Reading: The Development of Literacy in the Early Years of School*, London: Paul Chapman Publishing
This book tells the story of the research project, referred to in Chapters 3 and 4, that tracked the literacy development of children during their first year of school.

Tizard, B. (1993) 'Early influences on literacy', in Beard, R. (ed.) *Teaching Literacy Balancing Perspectives*, London, Sydney and Auckland: Hodder & Stoughton
This interesting chapter by Barbara Tizard, focusing on the reception year of school, summarises the findings of the Infant School Study.

The teaching of literacy 5

When you have read this chapter, you should:

- have revised the theoretical backgound that underpins the teaching of literacy

- know how an understanding of the literacy process can be translated into practice in the classroom

- be able to implement a balanced literacy programme in an early years class.

Teachers themselves have to be more knowledgeable and skilled about reading in order to teach it successfully.

(Ofsted, 1996)

The declared intention is for this series of books to be the companion volumes to the DfEE Circulars 10/97 and 4/98 and also for the accompanying documentation of the National Literacy Strategy *Framework for Teaching* (DfEE, 1998) implemented in September 1998 (see the series introduction, page ix). This book, therefore, aims to provide primary teacher educators, primary teachers and students with the knowledge, understanding and skills required to teach reading effectively and imaginatively in early years settings and classrooms. The intention is also to view reading in a wide frame of reference, ideologically dovetailed with writing and thus transformed into literacy and, crucially, as integral and interdependent with speaking and listening. This reaffirms belief in the ideology of the DfE (1995) documents of the National Curriculum for pupils. The inter-related nature of oracy and literacy is acknowledged throughout the book and is reinforced by the considered (and reconsidered!) order of the chapters.

The purpose of this chapter
The National Literacy Strategy *Framework for Teaching* provides teachers with a curriculum for teaching literacy throughout the primary school. The content is handled in detail and stipulates both

when (in terms of the year group and which point in the academic year) and also the *way* it is to be taught. The standardisation of the literacy curriculum with its deliberate prescription and detail, and, ground-breakingly for the UK, an accompanying pedagogy, will have an immense effect on the professionalism and practice of primary teachers. Whilst some will mourn the loss of the greater autonomy of the past, many will find the framework and the structure of the National Literacy Strategy supportive and enabling. Pupils, both those remaining in the same school and those who move from school to school, will benefit from the consistency of the one designated approach, and the clearly thought-out progression of content. The teaching of literacy has been removed beyond the realm of individual teacher opinion and chance into a canon to which virtually every school now must adhere.

So why the need for this book and this chapter, in particular, given the advent of such a clear government directive? The reasons are these. I have argued elsewhere (Riley, 1996) that teachers have to be knowledgeable about the processes involved in literacy so that they are able to teach children to become effective users of spoken and written language. Teachers are not technicians, they are professionals making complex and finely tuned judgements that inform their teaching. This volume aims to flesh out the theory referred to in the documents and which underpins current thinking on the teaching of reading. In so doing, it aims to fill the gaps that clearly exist in the *Framework for Teaching* so that teachers are better able to implement it with confidence and professional understanding.

This chapter aims to bring together the relevant understandings, which have been explored in depth earlier in the book, and, further, complementary practical skills to teach literacy in early years settings and classrooms. There will inevitably be some repetition from earlier chapters to avoid the need to refer back and forth in the book to obtain the necessary information. This chapter makes suggestions that complement and expand upon those of the National Literacy Strategy documents.

THEORIES UNDERPINNING THE TEACHING OF READING

This section looks briefly at theories of reading that have been discussed in depth earlier.

First and foremost, this chapter begins with the starting point that the child is a curious being and an efficent and active maker of meaning of all that she meets in the world and in her attempts to make sense of it. The mastery of spoken and written language are extraordinary examples of this apparently innate disposition to make meaning. It has been discussed, at length, how the meaning-making drives the acquisition of language and literacy, and how the different modes of language, namely speaking, listening, reading and writing, facilitate higher levels of thinking as the child strives to make sense of everything around her (see Chapters 1, 2, 3, 4 and 6). Language does this by enabling the individual to abstract, categorise, generalise and, through the generation of grammar, permits the acquisition and new manipulation of concepts.

Secondly, and because the child is such an effective agent in her own learning, it is essential that teachers are skilled diagnosticians of the overall development of each child's literacy stage and her prior learning before formal schooling and after. This is crucial so that teaching does not cut across previous learning and, in so doing, alienate and confuse the child and so waste time. In order that early years teachers are able to assess the child's literacy development accurately, they need to be very knowledgeable about the literacy task and the developmental stages of literacy through which the reader/writer must pass. In other words, both the psychological processes involved and the stages in the learning of literacy need to be thoroughly understood. There are two prerequisites that are necessary before successful teaching and learning of literacy can occur – one is a task for the child, the other is a task for the teacher.

The child's task

The reader has to first understand the purpose and conventions of print, and then to recognise that the alphabet is a code system.

Research into the emergent phase of literacy has charted the child's journey from the first glimmerings of print awareness to fluent reading and writing (see Chapter 4). The pre-school child becomes aware of writing as a rule-based system, and she realises that the purpose of written language is to communicate, that writing is a permanent and unchanging record of meaning and has a particular format, rules and conventions. These principles are all worked out by the child as a result of exposure to texts of many different kinds. The 'why' and 'how' of print, this gradual making sense of written language, is followed by the dawning realisation, through both teaching and experience, that the individual shapes, squiggles, curves and loops of the letters of the alphabet are distinct from each other and represent the different sounds of speech. The understanding of the symbolic nature of the alphabet is so crucial that no progress in literacy development can occur without it, however structured, colourful, imaginative and energetic the teaching of grapheme–phoneme (letter–sound) correspondence might be.

The adult's task

The teacher needs to understand what is involved in the literacy process and how best to support the development of the separate components of the process.

The stance taken in this book is that the reader makes sense of text through the means of a complex system of the mutually assisting and inter-related psychological *processes* (see the series introduction on page x, Chapters 2 and 3). Readers, both novice and experienced, need to use a blend of top-down and bottom-up processing in order to make sense of and to decode a text. The influence of the separate aspects of the processing system is more pronounced at different stages of proficiency and with different types of texts. An over-reliance in the use of one process seriously reduces fluency and the ability to make sense of the text. To read and write speedily and fluently, the reader has to be able to employ all the processes simultaneously and automatically. The different types of processing that occur are described in the National Literacy Strategy *Framework for Teaching* as the different *strategies* that the child uses in order to read text. The two terms, process and stategy, are not interchangeable or completely synonomous, but they both refer to the psychological operations that occur. Strategies are, in fact, the capacities to use the different cueing systems that the reader is able to employ when decoding. This is referred to in more detail later.

THE PSYCHOLOGICAL PROCESSES AT WORK WHEN READING

A method of teaching reading that aims to be comprehensive needs to draw on an explanation of the literacy process that accounts for its complexity. Figure 5.1 demonstrates the inter-relatedness of the different processes involved in diagramatic form.

Figure 5.1
The inter-relatedness of the reading process

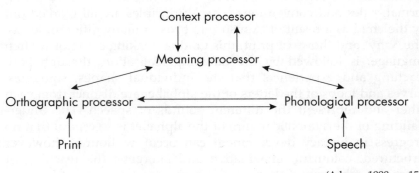

(Adams, 1990, p. 158)

How to develop top-down processing skills

It can be seen from Figure 5.1 that at the centre of the act of reading lies meaning-making, which fulfils the whole purpose of the activity. The context of the sentence or story supports the reader in the task of decoding in order to predict what the words might mean. This use of context is described as the top-down processing and is supported by the child's knowledge of the world, the story as a whole, the cover, the illustrations and the format of the book. The skills of prediction which are the product of top-down processing can be encouraged through introducing the book to the child, and when reading the story asking the child, for example, 'What do you think is going to happen now?' or 'What is she going to say to the Mother Bear?'.

The use of context cues also includes prediction about the kind of word that might be expected in the text according to the rules of language or grammar. In this instance, the adult might ask the child when she comes to an unknown word 'What do you think will make sense here?' or 'What sort of a word will fit here?' This way of working with even the youngest pupils reinforces to them the meaning gaining, active process that reading is.

How to develop bottom-up processing skills

Sound awareness

To learn to read, the child has also to be able to hear and distinguish between the different words and then to discriminate between the constituent sounds in words (phonemic segmentation). These are then decoded from the letters and groups of letters on the printed page. The child who has this ability is said to understand grapheme–phoneme (letter–sound) correspondence. This aspect of reading is demonstrated clearly in Figure 5.1.

An appreciation of both the visual aspects of print (orthographic processing) and the identification of the aural sounds of spoken language (phonological processing) develop side-by-side. The inter-relationship ensures that each complements the other – the development of one supports and reinforces the development of the other. This processing is referred to as the bottom-up or decoding skills. These skills can be developed not only through the adult sharing picture books with children, and so implicitly generating meaning from the printed text which includes drawing on the illustrations, but also through directly supporting the decoding aspect of reading. The experienced reader assists the novice by pointing to words as they are read aloud, directing attention to different words and pointing out those that are high-frequency, distinctive or highly patterned, for example, words that begin with the same letters as those in the child's name and are therefore easily identified by her. These approaches are incorporated in and described fully in the *Framework for Teaching* under the term 'shared reading'.

shared reading
where an adult and child(ren) work on a text together, the adult demonstrating and encouraging reading behaviours and skills

The bottom-up skills of phonological (sound) and orthographic (print) awareness are developed through both reading *and* writing, as the new school entrant gets to grips with both decoding and encoding as a literacy user. But a model of a teaching approach that takes into account, and is appropriate to, the child's literacy stage can powerfully assist progress (see Chapter 3).

Sound (phonological) awareness work will begin in the nursery and the *Framework for Teaching* provides details of the order in which the content should be taught. As discussed fully in Chapter 3, phonological awareness develops slowly and the child passes through stages on the way to being able to break up words accurately into phonemes (phonemic segmentation).

The first linguistic unit that young children appear to be able to distinguish spontaneously is rhyme (see Chapter 3 and Figure 3.1). Working with a small group of early readers, at approximately the same stage of phonological development, in order to focus on rhyme – for example, breaking words into the onset (initial phoneme) and rime (end phoneme), for example sh-*ook*, and then considering other words with the same endings b-*ook*, l-*ook*, t-*ook* – should take only a few minutes, and mainly when the children are writing. This can be very valuable, perhaps undertaken when **shared writing** is taking place during group teaching. Commercial and teacher-produced card and board games should be available for daily use in order to promote phonological awareness.

shared writing
adult and child(ren) working together on a writing task, eliciting wordings and spellings by appropriate prompts

Print awareness
The direct teaching of print (orthographic) awareness has first to be encouraged by thorough learning of the alphabet, perhaps through a published mnenomics scheme such as Letterland or Jolly Phonics, with games and rhymes, and also through plentiful, varied, attractive alphabet books and friezes. By the end of the reception year, children need to be able to both recognise and identify the upper and lower case letters of the alphabet, and also be able to reproduce them when writing, without constant recourse to an alphabet chart.

Next, the child builds up a sight vocabulary of high-frequency words of interest, words from the early reading books or on the current topic. The *Framework for Teaching* provides high-frequency word-lists and a suggested sequence of introduction to pupils in reception and Years 1 and 2. The memorisation of words which children will frequently meet in reading scheme books and words that will be needed when writing has great positive benefit. An increasingly large sight vocabulary speeds up reading and writing fluency, providing a basis of known words whenever a new text is met or is to be written. Energy is then released for decoding unknown words, employing all available cueing strategies when doing so. These words can be stored in individual word banks or folders for each child or in card pockets on a wall display and they should be in constant use for reference, cross-checking letter order and the patterns of letter strings in words, for practice and with games.

The rapid and accurate recognition of an increasing repertoire of the common keywords of text speeds progress towards fluent reading, once the child has grasped the purpose and usefulness of the literacy task. It is of *no value* whatever to begin too early or before the child has grasped conceptually what reading and writing are for and what literacy can do for human beings. Teaching words out of context, particularly before the child has any alphabetic decoding strategies at her disposal, results in the old hazards of the despised flash-card work from the enshrined practice of the 1960s and 1970s. It leads to stories such as the one about a 5-year-old child playing the flash-card game with her teacher, when defeated by the proffered card is unhelpfully prompted by an equally confused friend with 'Try DOG; it sometimes works'!

Teaching to support print recognition

Teachers of children in the early stages of learning to read have traditionally taught a list of high-frequency words in order to promote print awareness and to increase speed and fluency in both reading and writing. This practice went out of fashion for a while as it was seen to be too mechanistic and joyless an activity compared with the excitement of devouring challenging, stimulating texts!

Now, however, learning a sight vocabulary of high-frequency words, words of personal interest, words from the core reading scheme or the vocabulary of the class project, is enshrined in the practice of the *Framework for Teaching*, along with its lists of words (pages 60–3) to be memorised in progression through the reception, Years 1 and 2. Research evidence suggests that this is sound practice.

Chapter 3 discussed the fact that, for whole or sight words to be stored in an individual's lexicon (word memory bank), the words have to be 'learned' or seen so often that a logogen or 'picture' is created of them by the brain. The shape of the entire word can then be recalled when writing or recognised when reading, so that the meaning is also accessed from the individual's memory store. This process is achieved through developmental stages and is influenced by the refinement of sound (phonological) awareness to a greater or lesser extent, depending on your viewpoint or theoretical stance. There are stages through which the child passes on the way to fluent print processing. These have been discussed in depth in Chapter 3 but are outlined here again.

Frith's theory: the logographic phase of sight-word reading

In the first stage of print-processing described by Frith (1985), the young child perceives words as wholes or as logograms. The word is recognised by the child by personally memorable and highly distinctive visual features. The child has no recourse to phonological decoding as both letters of the alphabet and the associated sounds are not known or salient to the reader at this early stage of literacy development.

At this stage of sight-word reading, it is helpful if the teacher draws to the child's attention the salient features of text rather than relying on idiosyncratic mnemonic, as in the case of the child who knew it was television because of the two 'i's or the two sticks in lollipop – hardly the most useful strategy to use. Focusing attention to the letter–sound relationship with distinctive letters begins the use of more transferable strategies.

CASE STUDY

Attending to rhyme

A teacher is working with a group of 4-year-olds on the large poster (A3 size or larger) of the nursery rhyme of 'Humpty Dumpty'. After several joint readings/recitations, along with pointing and one-to-one matching of sound to word, she draws the children's attention to the two distinctive words H-*umpty* D-*umpty*. The words have different onsets and a common rime and, by drawing attention to the sound units matched to the written language, she develop children's print awareness.

1 What other activities could the teacher generate from the nursery rhyme 'Humpty Dumpty' to promote print and sound awareness?
2 Are there any pitfalls with words that are an aural rhyme but not a visual one, and so cause confusion, for example, *chair* and *pear*?

The alphabetic stage of sight-word reading

The child moves into the next phase of print processing as letters of the alphabet are learned by their distinguishing shapes, names or sounds. Ehri (1992) maintains that it is this knowledge that provides the child with sufficient 'low-level phonemic awareness' that the beginnings and ends of words can be recognised and rudimentary sound–spelling connections can be made. Words are still remembered by their distinctive shape details, but a crude sound–symbol link is also attached to the recognition process for the word and this is then effectively committed to the lexical memory store, or sight vocabulary. The pupil's early writing can be a useful indication that this stage of print processing has been reached, although production lags behind recognition.

At this stage the child will need to sight-learn the common function words by sight, such as 'went', 'play', 'on', 'in' and 'but', which make up 25 per cent of all text that the child will encounter at this stage of reading. These words tax the visual memory as they present no visual image to the child and are best learned by games which match phrases or sentences on a card to a reading book. Strips of card with the written phrases are matched under text by the child and then can be cut up, read, learned and re-assembled as a phrase.

The orthographic stage of sight-word reading

The reader is able to short-circuit the letter-by-letter phonological conversion of the previous stage through being able to process chunks of print (in the form of letter clusters or patterns) from sight memory. Parts of words are automatically processed from the lexical memory both to encode and decode, and the child speeds up when reading and spelling becomes more regular. Fluency is improved as decoding becomes almost instantaneous.

The more reading a child undertakes and the more fluent she becomes, the greater her sight vocabulary or memory bank will be. Fewer words will need decoding afresh each time they are encountered. Sight words are stored in the reader's lexical memory bank and can be recalled instantaneously when perceived and are often recalled along with the phrases and patterns of written language in which they occur. This literacy knowledge is not acquired simply through learning by rote, perhaps particularly *not* by learning by rote! Reading is an active process and the brain has to process words thoroughly by perceiving, comprehending and using, not *just* memorising. In the same way, when learning a foreign language, a vocabulary list can be remembered after a period of time only with actual use and that is most powerfully achieved in the relevant country.

How a sight vocabulary is acquired

Early years teachers can support print awareness and the development of a sight vocabulary through offering their pupils opportunities to:

- read many types of text on different subjects with rich patterns of language and which capitalise on repetition and rhythm
- write with adult support on a variety of topics for many purposes (shared writing, see *Implications for practice* on page 101)
- attend to words in and out of context, common words in environmental print, children's names, labels, notices and signs
- use word folders and banks when writing and when playing word games
- have the words from the NLS high-frequency word lists drawn to their attention when reading continuous texts

and by:

- using the language experience approach to literacy which converts spoken language into writing in the child's presence and explicitly reinforces letter–sound relationships and the patterns and structures of words.

Regarding the rationale on the learning of high-frequency words the *Framework for Teaching* says:

> they are essential high frequency words which pupils will need, even to tackle very simple texts. These words usually play an important part in holding together the general coherence of texts and early familiarity with them will help pupils get pace and accuracy into their reading at an early stage. Some of the words have irregular or difficult spellings and, because they often play an important grammatical part, they are hard to predict from the surrounding text.

(DfEE, 1998, p. 80)

It is expected by the authors of the *Framework for Teaching* that 45 words should be learned in the reception year and 150 words in Years 1 and 2. This ambitious target will support reading and writing of new texts considerably.

The National Literacy Strategy model of the literacy process

Figure 5.1 and its following explanation is a helpful explanatory model for early years teachers. It provides insight into what occurs in the brain when reading, an insight which is an essential starting point for their teaching. The National Literacy Strategy *Framework for Teaching* uses a slightly different model (see Figure 5.2) which, whilst it provides information mainly in explanation of the cueing system that is available to the reader, does not demonstrate the importance of meaning being at the centre of the process, or the mutually reinforcing roles of print and sound awareness.

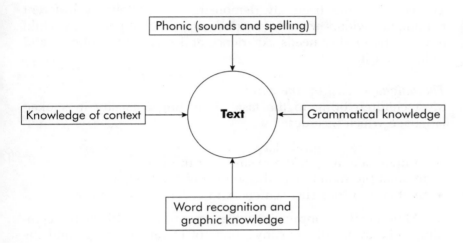

Figure 5.2
The headlamps searching text to inform the reader

(DfEE, 1998, p. 4)

Figure 5.2 is an amalgamation of Figure 5.1, and the Clay and Cazden (1990) diagram (Figure 3.3) describing the strategies (or cueing systems) used by the reader in order to make sense of text. It has been discussed at length that all four of these cueing systems need to be operating for fast, fluent reading.

The stage of literacy development as a starting point

An awareness of the beginner reader's development, what she understands and can do, is essential before effective teaching can occur. Given that reading involves a system of perceptual and cognitive operations, it is the task of the adult working with the child to analyse the outward, observable signs that indicate the processing that is occurring.

Clay (1991) has described how, through knowledgeable, skilled observation of the child when reading, the teacher is able to assess the behaviours displayed and the strategies the child employs in order to read an unknown word. For the purposes of this book, an unknown word can be described as one that is not in her sight vocabulary and has to be decoded. Clay describes this notion as 'sensitive observation while teaching' (1991, p. 232)

This is not a principle that is new to any early years teacher, the adage 'observe, support, extend' is a fundamental part of the professional repertoire.

Behaviour that should be noted

The complex and fleetingly demonstrated repertoire of different reading behaviours which show understanding on part of the child is vast. The teacher needs experience and practice to notice it and to interpret it.

The language used by the child

Most children bring to the task of reading a facility in spoken language which includes:

- a wide range of vocabulary
- an understanding of the meaning of the words
- an ability to manipulate the sounds of the language
- an ability to construct sentences to order to communicate.

In addition to these impressive achievements, the child will be beginning to be aware of the conventions of literary language and the patterns and rhythm of oral language. Teachers will notice the influence of the child's oral language in her early attempts to read and write. Competent use of oral language has within it the basis of the child's ability to predict words when reading, through her deep knowledge of language structures and meanings.

Understanding of the conventions of print

The early stages of learning to read involve becoming aware of concepts about print and realising that it is necessary to pay attention to them. These include:

- the appreciation of directionality of text
- the spaces between words and lines
- formats, punctuation and the general features of continuous text.

Consolidation of these understandings occurs slowly over the first year of school and leads to more refined understandings of metalanguage and the understanding of a letter, a word and a sentence.

Awareness of visual information

This includes early orthographic awareness as children explore patterns of print in highly personal ways. (See Chapter 3 and earlier in this chapter.)

Hearing sounds in sequence in words
This involves the development of phonological awareness. (See Chapter 3 and earlier in this chapter.)

The sources of information about text that the child is able to employ to make sense of it, as described above, are demonstrated clearly in Figure 3.3.

THE ASSESSMENT AND RECORDING OF LITERACY PROGRESS

A well-developed ability to monitor and assess progress in literacy is essential when working with a child who is delayed in reading development or confused about certain aspects of literacy. I would argue that the observant and knowledgeable teacher has a huge advantage over her less-informed colleagues when teaching beginner readers. The potential for the young child's progress to be erratic or unbalanced is immense, given the complexity of the literacy process. This is before the issue of individual learning styles or particular difficulties are considered. Therefore the monitoring of development is very important.

The main reasons for regularly monitoring the literacy progress of pupils are to:

- establish what each child can do
- identify what strategies each is using
- assess the individual child's stage and rate of development
- enable the teacher to provide appropriate teaching and tasks for the individual and/or small groups
- inform the choice of the appropriate materials
- ensure appropriate organisational strategies are used, for example, the different grouping of children.

Monitoring follows the 'assess, plan, teach, assess' cycle of primary teaching and is integral to the programme for literacy. It needs to be carried out at regular intervals – many theorists suggest every three or four weeks for those pupils making average progress. Children with difficulties need to be assessed more frequently.

Monitoring can occur at different levels during normal teaching sessions. Class organisation can be arranged so that there is opportunity to assess one or two children daily.

Formal monitoring follows assessment on arrival at school (see Chapter 4). Experienced teachers constantly observe children across all types of activity in order to monitor learning and this diagnostic observation informs teaching.

Formal monitoring involves assessing and recording the child's development regarding:

- the attitudes to literacy and ability to concentrate
- the essential understandings about print and its conventions
- the strategies used when reading continuous text.

Specific skills and abilities that need to be assessed are:

- how well directionality and one-to-one (i.e. written word to spoken word) matching are established
- the extent to which the child uses strategies of predicting, confirming and self-correction
- the child's appropriate use of available cues
- the extent to which the child's use of cues is integrated
- the ability with which the child is able to reconstruct meaning of the text
- the extent of the child's sight vocabulary
- the child's ability to hear sounds in words (i.e. whether she can segment phonemes) and to map the sounds onto a symbol or group of symbols, with increasing accuracy in appreciation of the vagaries of the English language
- the stage of the child's writing development in particular with invented spellings.

Holdaway's advice is still sound. He says:

> *the best policy is to monitor actual behaviour as the child carries out the task in a meaningful situation – such as normal reading and writing within the programme – and to compare such observations with those taken for the same child at some previous time.*

(Holdaway, 1979, p. 168)

miscue analysis
a verbatim record of a child's reading and analysis of the miscues to identify the strategies being used and future needs

running reading record
a quantative and qualitative analysis of the child's reading to identify the progress being made and cueing systems being used

A teacher's observation of one or two children daily through undertaking of **miscue analysis** or **running reading record** ensures that all the pupils in the class are formally assessed approximately once a month. Such records, when completed regularly and systematically, monitor reading (processing) behaviour as the reader is working on an unfamiliar text, in order to build up a picture of development. Pupils who cause concern may need more frequent monitoring. Children progress at different rates from each other and are at different stages of development. Class teachers need to be aware of the variations within and between pupils, to ensure that the class provision matches their constantly changing literacy needs.

Running reading records and miscue analysis

Running reading records and miscue analysis are methods of assessing reading behaviour and recording the level of accuracy on an unfamiliar text, largely unaided. In addition, they use the child's errors (miscues) to determine her processing abilities as she utilises the cues available to her. In other words, they are systematic frameworks for observation that enable the knowledgeable teacher to capture and record the behaviours that indicate the print-processing that the child is able to employ when reading a text.

Issues regarding the choice of texts

When undertaking an observation of a child's reading, the choice of the text is important. If the child finds a text too easy, it means that she is reading most of the words from her sight vocabulary. A text that is too difficult means that she is not able to read a sufficient number of the words to be able to benefit from top-down (meaning-making) processing to inform the bottom-up (decoding) processing of the text. In other words, the text becomes so full of gaps, as many of the words are ignored, that there is no opportunity for the child to be able to predict a word using overall sense, context or syntax cues.

The levels of text difficulty

Difficulty of texts can be determined through the child being able to read the following proportions of the passage (Clay, 1993, p. 23):

- an easy text (95 to 100 per cent correct)
- an instructional text (90–94 per cent correct)
- a hard text (80–90 per cent correct).

The running reading record is most useful for teachers of children at the beginning stages of reading because it provides opportunity both to analyse the errors or miscues for the reasons cited above and also to estimate the child's performance quantatively and so monitor progress. This is achieved only if a school has the reading books organised in a structured progression of difficulty which enables teachers to determine the appropriateness of the reading book in terms of a match between a child's reading ability to text difficulty in a systematic way.

Undertaking a running reading record

The approach to taking a running reading record (not a running record as my students call them – as if we are fitness freaks!) is to practise and then to practise some more. The conventions are the most difficult aspect of the record to use well and the observation aspect requires expertise, obviously, but mainly experience.

Figure 5.3a

An example of a running reading record

RUNNING RECORD SHEET

Name: *Joanna*   Date: *9-11-95*   D. of B.: _____   Age: ____ yrs ____ mths

School: _____   Recorder: _____

Text Titles	Running words / Error	Error rate	Accuracy	Self-correction rate
1. Easy _____	_____	1: _____	_____ %	1: _____
2. Instructional _____	_____	1: _____	_____ %	1: _____
3. Hard *The toys' party*	*48⁄5*	1: *9*	*89* %	1: *2*

Directional movement _____

Analysis of Errors and Self-corrections
Information used or neglected [Meaning (M) Structure or Syntax (S) Visual (V)]

Easy _____

Instructional _____

Hard *Joanna was paying close attention to the storyline throughout, and made good use of her strong oral language. She attended to print cues variably.*

Cross-checking on information (Note that this behaviour changes over time)
Additional print information and flexible attention to meaning led Joanna to correct half her errors.

Analysis of Errors and Self-corrections
(see *Observation Survey* pages 30–32)

Page	The toys' party				E	SC	Information used E MSV	SC MSV
1	✓	✓	✓	✓				
2	*Every / Nobody* | SC	✓	✓	*make / come*	1	1	Ⓜ Ⓢ V / Ⓜ Ⓢ V	Ⓜ S Ⓥ
4	✓	✓	✓	*teddies / toys* | SC		1	Ⓜ Ⓢ Ⓥ	M S Ⓥ
6	✓̌	*went / wanted* | R | SC	✓	*birthday*	✓	1 / 1	Ⓜ Ⓢ Ⓥ / Ⓜ Ⓢ V	M S Ⓥ
8	✓	✓	✓	*cocopops / cornflakes* | A | T		1	Ⓜ Ⓢ Ⓥ	
9	✓	✓	✓	✓	*ketchup / sauce*	1	Ⓜ Ⓢ V	
10	✓	✓	✓	✓				

Practice makes perfect! The more records that teachers undertake, the more subtle the behaviour that will be noticed. An example of a running reading record is shown in Figures 5.3a and 5.3b. Advice on how to conduct a running reading record is provided in the Appendix on page 176 and is taken from Clay (1993, pp 24, 27, 28 and 29).

Figure 5.3b

Page		E	SC	Analysis of Errors and Self-corrections (see *Observation Survey* pages 30–32) Information used — E MSV	SC MSV
11	✓ ✓ ✓ ✓				
12	✓ ✓ ✓ ✓				
13	✓ ✓ ✓ beans | SC / baked		1	Ⓜ Ⓢ Ⓥ	M S Ⓥ
14	✓ saw | SC / was angry / cross	1	1	Ⓜ Ⓢ Ⓥ / Ⓜ Ⓢ V	Ⓜ Ⓢ Ⓥ
16	✓ ✓ ✓				

The toys' party. Oxford Reading Tree Stage 2

1. Kipper wanted a party.
2. Nobody wanted to come.
4. He got his toys.
6. He wanted a cake.
8. He put in cornflakes.
9. He put in tomato sauce.
10. He put in milk.
11. He put in jam.
12. He put in sugar.
13. He put in baked beans.
14. Mum was cross.
16. Kipper was sorry.

(Riley, 1996, using the format suggested in Clay, 1993, p. 25)

Assessment of knowledge of the alphabetic code through writing

Early mark-making attempts have the advantage for the teacher that they are, unlike reading, a permanent record of the child's print-processing abilities. Writing is the mirror image of reading in that it is the encoding of the spoken word into written language. In reading, the goal is to access meaning which is achieved through strategies of whole-word shape, context and decoding by grapheme–phoneme and orthographic processing. Writing is often letter-by-letter grapho-motor production. Both processes contribute to literacy acquisition. Writing develops slightly behind reading, although they are complementary to each other.

Clay (1993) talks about very early mark-making as being an exploration of literacy and describes the process that children go through as a pathway:

> *from scribble to letter-like forms, to letter-like shapes, often part of their own name, to favourite letters and particular words. . .all the time invented forms and invented words intrude into productions as they explore possibilities.*
>
> (Clay, 1993, p. 11)

These early attempts demonstrate the child struggling to grasp the conventions of print, as well as the beginnings of letter–sound knowledge.

As the child writes, she actively struggles with the orthographic and phonological processors (see Figure 5.1) as she converts the sounds she can hear in parts of words into symbols on the paper with invented spelling (i.e. the writer is inventing and working out for herself the sound–symbol correspondences and is not being provided with words to copy, with a personal dictionary or with a *Breakthrough to Literacy* folder [Mackay *et al.*, 1970]). This approach to writing provides the teacher with a crucially important opportunity to analyse literacy development.

When she is inventing spellings, the child tends to move through stages of development (Gentry, 1981) which gradually become more refined and conventional. These are:

- pre-communication
- semi-phonetic
- phonetic
- transitional.

Pre-communication

At this stage the young writer is indicating that she knows that symbols can represent speech for a given purpose. The writing will be a rough approximation of known letters or numbers. Often the letters of her own name are used repeatedly and in random order.

Semi-phonetic
One-, two- and three-letter spellings, at this stage, show some representation of letter–sound (grapheme–phoneme) correspondence, for example, 'wnt' for 'went', 'dg' for 'dog', 'p' for 'please'.

Phonetic
Now the writer has almost perfect grapheme–phoneme match as she develops the ability to phonologically segment words, for example, 'becos' for 'because', 'wot' for 'what', 'sed' for 'said', 'wen' for 'when'.

Transitional
At this stage of literacy development, the child is in the orthographic stage of reading and able to process groups of letters without letter-by-letter conversion. In writing she is able to move gradually towards conventional spelling. The ability to process chunks of words enables a recognition of the 'look' of a word to be remembered, and familiar patterns from a working sight vocabulary can be utilised but imperfectly, for example, 'huose' for 'house', 'eightee' for 'eighty', 'thay' for 'they'.

In this stage the child begins to appreciate that in English the same sound can be represented by different groups of letters, for example, *ay, ai* or *a. . .e.* If the child is encouraged to use invented spelling she will demonstrate her developing awareness of:

- alphabet and letter names
- letter–sound relationships.

When writing on her own the child demonstrates other understandings, such as:

- directional rules
- concepts of a letter or a word
- the functions of space
- the ordering of letters in a word
- the sequence of sounds within a word
- punctuation.

Implications for practice
The teaching approach of shared writing capitalises on the experimental and self-directed nature of this mark-making and early writing. It is necessary to support further progress by scaffolding the child's encoding at exactly the appropriate moment. A teacher

working either on shared texts, or with children working on their own texts in small groups with four or five pupils at similar stages of development, is an effective way of enabling print–sound connections to be reinforced. Modelling writing with use of a white board or an easel is helpful. Close observation of the writing as it is being generated letter-by-letter enables support to be given at exactly the right moment. Too early intervention and essential problem-solving is curtailed; too delayed and the child has moved on to the next word and the moment of focused attention and decision-making is lost. Assistance with breaking a word into its constituent sounds and then support and direction to the symbol (i.e. letter or the choice between two letters) on an alphabet strip that represents that sound are very valuable.

For some children, support at this stage of writing is only needed for a very short time, for others such directed and focused teaching is required for longer until they genuinely have grasped the alphabetic code as a system. For these children this activity should be a frequent one and planned within the Literacy Hour group activities.

ASSESSMENT OF ATTITUDES TO READING

Assessment of the child's processing of text is only part of the picture of literacy development that the early years teacher needs for each of her pupils. Teachers need also to be aware of how enthusiastic the child is about reading, which books she chooses to look at or work with, which types of books she enjoys, as well as her levels of concentration span and motivation. This insight into the child's informal knowledge, skills, interests and attitudes about reading is important from the perspective of the child as a reader in a wider sense.

Awareness of the overall literacy profile is achieved through the observation of the child in many different circumstances and situations. These might be:

- noting enjoyment of and involvement with books, stories and story times
- noticing the books the child chooses to look at when not directed
- talking to the child about a particular book and ascertaining her views of her own reading development (such self-evaluation is often very informative)
- observing a child during shared or group reading, noting levels of engagement and participation
- asking parents about the child's level of interest when reading at home

- noting the type and frequency of written records kept by parents in connection with the home–school reading scheme. This will reveal a great deal about the emphasis placed on literacy and the messages given to children daily at home about learning to read.

Record-keeping

The observation data of the type described is informative and useful for the class teacher – to inform planning, teaching and grouping of children for teaching purposes. All documentation kept on individual pupils needs to be manageable and of potential value to the class teacher. Reviewing of records needs to be built into the school policy to establish the rate of progress being made. Systematic and regularly kept records ensure that progress is monitored for all the pupils and provides evidence on the fast, average and slow learners in literacy.

A language and literacy profile

A language and literacy profile might take the form of a folder for each pupil containing the following records:

- school entry checklist/baseline assessment
- running reading records (completed approximately every four weeks), including analysis of the observations and notes on levels of comprehension and discussion of the stories read
- title and level of difficulty of books read
- notes on any discussion with parents and home–school records
- dated, annotated samples of the child's writing
- brief notes of conversations with child about her reading, especially those that denote interests and attitudes.

Summary

The aim of this chapter has been to complete the picture presented by the National Literacy Strategy *Framework of Teaching* by offering a balanced and informed approach to the teaching of literacy. The place of assessment and monitoring of progress has been discussed, as well as the purpose of teaching to develop a sight vocabulary and sound awareness.

The key points that have been addressed in this chapter are:

- **the processes involved in reading**

- **the teaching that is required to support the development of these processes**

- **the monitoring of reading progress.**

Further reading

Bielby, N. (1998) *How to Teach Reading: A Balanced Approach,* Leamington Spa: Scholastic
A useful book on how to develop further children's reading strategies, written by a literacy specialist with Key Stage 2 experience. See also the book in this series *Teaching Reading at Key Stage 2* by Nicholas Bielby.

Browne, A. (1998) *A Practical Guide to Teaching Reading in the Early Years,* London: Paul Chapman Publishing
This is exactly what it says, a practical guide, and has a valuable whole-class perspective. See also the book in this series *Teaching Writing at Key Stage 1 and Before* by Ann Browne.

Children who find learning to read difficult 6

When you have read this chapter, you should:

- understand the complexity of the nature of learning difficulty

- be aware of the importance of early diagnosis

- be aware of the different types of intervention programmes

- be able to implement a classroom-based programme for a delayed reader.

Introduction

Reading affects everything that you do.

(Stanovich, 1986)

A volume devoted to the teaching of reading would be seriously flawed without a section that addresses the relatively small, but significant, group of children who find learning to read difficult.

Both professionally and personally I have known children who entered the reception class reading fluently or, once there, appeared to learn to read as if by magic, with minimal support. Appropriate, differentiated teaching is essential for children who learn to read rapidly and easily so that they maintain their headstart and continue to progress in keeping with their ability.

Children develop and learn at very different rates and a wide range can be found in what might be considered 'normal' development. This being true, however, in every class, in every school, there will be a varying small percentage of pupils (10–20 per cent) who do not progress in literacy in line with their peers. Marie Clay, the originator of the Reading Recovery Programme, which now operates over most of the English-speaking world, predicts that, however effective the teaching programme in mainstream schooling, there will be a minority of pupils who will be in need of recognition and additional support with learning to read and write.

WHY SOME CHILDREN DO NOT BENEFIT FROM CLASS TEACHING PROGRAMMES

Clay (1992) suggests that we can always find a 'tail' of under-achievement in any classroom setting, because:

> *Children differ from one another in intelligence, language, cultural, organic or psychological competencies that interact with learning.*
>
> *Some children do not achieve well in our classrooms because they cannot come to grips with the setting and the culture of the classroom, or with our teaching or the tasks we set them.*
>
> *The first year of school is a time of many sicknesses and absences, and the individual lives of children are full of dramas and crises.*
>
> *Once we begin to teach children we create differences between them in rates of progress. . .*

(Clay, 1992, p. 71)

Given that we have spent the five previous chapters considering the complexity of the reading process, it is small wonder that some children will have problems with its mastery. Educational psychologists have drawn up frameworks that explain the inter-related nature of learning problems, of which difficulty in learning to read is often the one that causes the most distress and concern.

Blagg (1981) considers that the factors that affect the child's ability to learn, namely the physical, cognitive, social and emotional factors, and also those that affect attitude and learning style, present a problem that needs to be viewed within a broad theoretical frame-work. Blagg suggests that this framework should encompass the dimensions of the situation from a *within the family, within the child* and *within the school* perspective.

This kind of inter-related framework reminds the early years teacher that the cause of a difficulty is rarely unitary and, if not addressed from a multi-faceted point of view, the various separate factors multiply in their effect on the child's functioning. The underlying cause of the learning difficulty can seen to be exacerbated or amelio-rated by the child's home and school situation in the following case studies.

THREE CASE STUDIES

Winston

Six-year-old Winston is the youngest of a family of five children all of whom attend the local primary school. He is regularly absent from class and, when he does attend, he is often late for school due to the pressure experienced by his mother in getting all the children out in the mornings. Winston is a friendly, rather vague little boy. He has integrated rather superficially into school. He is happy enough to be there, but without any real engagement or positive contribution to discussions or the life of the class. He appears to be happiest when working with construction materials particularly 'big bricks' or playing in the home corner on his own. After 14 months of school, Winston has made little progress with reading and writing. His parents are beginning to be concerned.

Analysis of Winston's 'problem'
Winston knows books are for pleasure and information. He has acquired some of the concepts about print and recognises a few letters of the alphabet, but he is unsure of the sounds that they make and is still at the scribble writing stage of mark-making.

- *Within the child*: Due to poor attendance and the frequent late arrivals, Winston feels slightly on the outside of the school situation. In addition, he frequently misses the explanation to 'tune' him in to the tasks and teaching at the start of the day.
- *Within the family*: Winston is the youngest child in a slightly chaotic, disorganised, noisy family situation. He has had little individual attention from an adult before school. His speech development was delayed, but not at the level of clinical concern, due to the lack of one-to-one conversations of the quality and type that promote language development (see Chapter 1). Following on from this, Winston's pre-school experience of print, books and stories was limited and he came into reception class with only vague notions of texts and print and the way that they work. His home life also has given him few opportunities to develop the ability to learn how to learn, to concentrate and to focus on sedentary tasks.
- *Within the school*: The teacher is newly qualified and only just coping with the organisation of the learning for the 30 other pupils in her class. She is caring, but has not fully come to grips with being able to differentiate work for her class, so she reluctantly leaves Winston to the primary assistant who works with him on his reading and writing. The relative inexperience of the class teacher means that she has not fully assessed Winston and so been unable to analyse exactly what he knows and does not know about literacy. Therefore she is not aware of what he needs to learn before progress can be made. This needs to occur before any additional teaching approaches and resources can be considered.

What do you consider to be the main priority in Winston's case?

continued...

Bernice

Bernice is 5 years old. She is a happy but rather disobedient little girl. She appears to ignore instructions, frequently not completing the tasks set for her. The class teacher, who is very experienced, is concerned that after two terms in the reception class Bernice is making no connections between print and sound either when reading or writing.

Analysis of Bernice's difficulty
She enjoys stories and looking at books and has acquired most of the concepts about print. She can identify and label the letters of the alphabet by name. Her reading is accomplished through memorising the text and a small sight vocabulary. She makes no attempt to word-build. Her independent writing is still at the scribble writing stage or with the random use of letters.

- *Within the child*: During her three terms there, it was recorded that Bernice was absent frequently from the nursery with upper-respiratory infections. Through one-to-one conversations with the child, the reception teacher has had opportunity to pick up on a possible hearing difficulty. A referral to the school medical service resulted in a diagnosis of glue ear. This condition can cause varying degrees of hearing loss. The deafness, although often intermittent in nature, blunts auditory discrimination. This, in turn, affects reading progress, particularly in the early stages. Typically the child is often unable to distinguish aurally between man, mad and mat.
- *Within the family*: Bernice comes from a relaxed family who believe in children being supported with their education, but not pressured. They share the books with her from the home–school reading scheme but are not concerned about the way she is progressing.
- *Within the school*: Bernice's class occupies a large room, adjacent to the parallel reception class with a shared resouces area for painting, model-making and construction. On occasions, there are 50 or 60 children working in the area as a whole. The noise levels are high.

1 What is the main issue in this situation?
2 What should the class teacher do after the medical condition has been remedied?

Adam

Adam has been in school for two years and, at 7, he has made only a beginning with reading. He writes very little and when he does it is ill-formed, and his invented spelling shows little letter–sound correspondence. His class teacher is puzzled as he is articulate with a good general knowledge, he loves stories and looking at books and is average at mathematics. Adam's parents are now very anxious as his younger brother in the reception class is progressing more rapidly than Adam on the school reading scheme.

continued...

Analysis of Adam's 'problem'

- *Within the child:* Adam came to school with high expectations. He was very motivated to read, coming from a family in which books and literacy are given high status. Once at school, Adam had difficulties making letter–sound connections in both reading and writing. He has acquired a small sight vocabulary of 20 or so words, which he can recognise when reading, but can only spell about five of them. He has problems distinguishing between some letters of the alphabet (for example, d/b, g/p and m/n/h) and in remembering the sequence of the letters in words even, on occasions, in his own second name. His visual and aural memory are poor. He is able to predict words from the global and local context well.
- *Within the family:* Initially Adam's parents worked hard with him on his reading, reading books with him several times to practise. The comparison with his younger brother has now made Adam's parents increasingly worried. The relationship between the two boys is fast becoming an issue, and Adam is beginning to be naughty at both home and school.
- *Within the school:* For two years Adam has been taught within the school literacy programme. The previous teacher identified a learning difficulty but, after some extra reading help and when some progress was made, she had considered that Adam would soon catch up. The current class teacher believes that the time has come for Adam to be formally assessed by the educational psychologist.

1 What do you think is the most worrying aspect of Adam's problem?
2 What makes Adam different from Bernice?
3 Would the same teaching in class be useful to them both?

These case studies indicate clearly how learning difficulties are often multi-factorial and the more dimensions to a problem there are, the greater the disabling effect of each one becomes. In other words the separate influence of each factor is multiplied several times, as the impact accumulates one on the other. Conversely, a difficulty such as **dyslexia** or a hearing loss, due to **glue ear**, can be compensated for by an enabling, supportive home and school situation.

FACTORS INVOLVED IN LITERACY DIFFICULTIES

Children who are making a slow start with learning to read and write may be experiencing one or several of the following difficulties relating to:

- physical factors
- social and emotional factors
- cognitive factors
- attitudes and learning style.

dyslexia
literally, difficulty with reading; a complex syndrome in which the child has visual and aural perceptual and sequencing difficulties

glue ear
a medical condition in which repeated ear infections have resulted in a build-up of a thick, glue-like liquid in the inner ear

Physical factors

Physical factors affect children's ability to benefit from the school programme. The state of a child's general health affects enthusiasm, concentration and receptiveness to learning opportunities. The adequacy of hearing, eyesight, speech and motor skills affect literacy development in obvious and direct ways. Following the diagnosis of a physical impairment, the learning environment may need to be adapted, with the addition of specialised equipment. In the case of hearing loss, a reduction of extraneous background noise might need to be considered.

In Bernice's case, her deafness is relatively easy to remedy through medical intervention. Drainage tubes placed into the inner ear to keep it free of liquid will restore hearing.

Social and emotional factors

Social and emotional factors have great potential to either boost or damage a child's personal coping mechanisms. Certain personality characteristics, such as sensitivity, confidence, maturity, sociability, stress tolerance, and so on, in either the parents or the child will affect the quality of their relationship and the bond between them. This, in turn, influences the child's perception of self-worth, and feeling supported and valued. Children with poor self-esteem have notoriously low reserves of perseverance and risk-taking, which reduce their success in any learning situation, but in the huge challenge that learning to read presents it can be completely disabling.

Cognitive factors

Cognitive factors cover a range of abilities, such as receptive and expressive language skills, verbal and non-verbal reasoning ability, visual and auditory perceptual skills, visual and auditory long- and short-term memory functions. The literacy-specific skills of phonological and orthographic processing are included as a subset within these. This will be expanded upon later.

Dyslexia, or specific learning difficulty, is included in this category of learning difficulty. Adam, in our case study, is an example of this type of specific learning difficulty.

Attitudes and learning style

These factors have a great potential to influence the child's capacity to learn to read. The positive attitudes of parents towards education, literacy and their expectations of and for the child are key features to her success at school.

Through these parental attitudes, the child's own confidence, interest and expectations are moulded and rebound on the learning situation for good or ill. The qualities of persistence and concentration are determined through being offered role models and satisfying, enriching literacy opportunities, both at home and at school, which reinforce a sense of the worthwhile nature of the task.

This consideration of the underlying causes of any learning difficulty reinforces the nature of the demands made on class teachers, especially those in their first years of teaching. Nevertheless, a professional accountability clearly exists.

EARLY DIAGNOSIS OF LITERACY DIFFICULTIES

The Code of Practice for children with special educational needs (DfEE, 1994) firmly places the initial responsibility for helping children with literacy difficulties with the school. It therefore behoves the class teacher to be aware of children who are not making expected progress, first at school entry and then through the continuous assessment of pupils. This enhances the class teacher's ability to be proactive in implementing an appropriate programme of differentiated teaching.

The conscious and public recognition of slower than 'normal' progress is problematic for most early years teachers. Not only may they be unwilling to label pupils as having a 'problem', but they may wish to give very young children a chance to adjust to the school system and to mature as learners. Winston's case, in the case studies, could have been easily argued this way and it was what actually occurred in the example of Adam.

However, early detection and action is important on many counts.

- It is essential that confusions are quickly resolved. Early deviant literacy behaviour can become entrenched and is much harder to rectify later.
- An early successful start to literacy sets the child on the path to academic achievement – learning to read becomes reading to learn and access to the whole curriculum is curtailed by an inability to read.
- A sense of competence and self-esteem is easily bruised and affects the whole of the child's functioning.
- Early intervention often makes complete recovery possible and renders unnecessary expensive remedial support later in school life.

Detection of difficulty

Even an inexperienced teacher will become concerned about a reception class child if no progress has been made between the first assessment on admission, and the next, that occurs after a few weeks in school (see Chapters 2 and 3). Most children will have developed from the baseline assessment in terms of confidence and conceptual understandings about print and with texts. Teachers will recognise the progress that has been made in some or all of the following measures.

Early literacy behaviours

These include:

- ability to talk about stories and their illustrations
- awareness of the concepts about print
- knowledge of letter names and sounds
- ability to hear and separate sounds in words
- ability to write her own name and a few words
- the ability to concentrate for longer periods.

All these skills and concepts develop once the receptive child is in a formal school literacy programme. If a difficulty is noticed, however minor or potentially transient, the class teacher needs to discuss the child with the Special Educational Needs Co-ordinator (SENCO). Monitoring alone may occur for a short passage of time or the next step may be taken immediately.

More extensive and specific assessment is undertaken if and when it is considered appropriate to establish the nature and extent of the literacy difficulty, perhaps on the lines of the Clay (1993) Observation Survey. The next stage, which is at the first level of the Special Needs Code of Conduct, is to record the concern, following the requirements of the school or LEA policy, and to inform the parents officially, who should then be invited to come to school to discuss the situation.

What needs to happen next? Views and individual situations vary.

Different views of remedial teaching

Earlier (see the series introduction, page x) and elsewhere (Riley, 1996), I have argued that for teachers to be effective teachers of literacy they need to have a clear idea of the psychological processes involved. It follows that, when children begin to experience difficulties with learning to read and write, the class teacher needs to have not only an understanding of the literacy process but also an idea of what is going amiss with the processing. In addition, she needs to be well informed about the approaches that experimental psychology tells us are effective in enabling the child to make progress.

If we consider the Adams model of the literacy process (Figure 5.1, page 86) and the view that, in order to read fluently, the individual has to have in place effective top-down and bottom-up processing of text, the question is, which of these is most likely to be faulty when the child fails to learn to read. Traditional remedial methods answer the question with a very clear and loud answer that the fault lies with the 'bottom-up' skills and that these have not been learned thoroughly. Commonly, in junior schools and secondary remedial departments, the methods of teaching adopted are over-whelmingly phonic instruction approaches such as Alpha and Omega, covering the 1,001 ways to teach letter–sound relationships. This approach results in varying degrees of success for probably a number of reasons. The children, being older, have struggled for longer, have lost heart and often have fallen behind their peers with all their work. Despite these additional considerations, a programme of phonics and more phonics does not appear to be the whole answer.

Reading Recovery

Other systems of support adopt a top-down and a more holistic approach of intervention. Reading Recovery is a school-based early intervention system for very young children who are beginning to fall behind their peers. It has been designed for all the reasons cited earlier. Reading Recovery works on a 'prevention being better than cure' principle and it is highly effective (Hurry, 1995). Hobsbaum (1997) maintains that 80 per cent of the children who enter the programme are able to rejoin their classes as capable readers and writers in approximately 20 weeks, and that only one child in five in this group of delayed learners will need further support. It is undeniably expensive on two fronts. Firstly, the teachers have to be trained into the programme. Secondly, children in the Reading Recovery programme need half an hour of daily one-to-one tuition for between 12 to 20 weeks. It is argued, however, that this cost is minimal compared to statementing an older child and instating remedial teaching higher up the school. Certainly, it is possible to justify Reading Recovery on humanitarian grounds alone.

Clay describes the programme as one that:

> *was developed from an interactionist view of reading (reading continuous text), based on information theory which emphasises how knowledge, strategies and processes at each level of language organisation expand and become interrelated (Clay, 1992).*

> *What the child knows about letters, sounds, syntax, meanings, stories and various kinds of texts is at first applied to reading and writing tasks in rather separate and unrelated ways. With use these bodies of knowledge develop links and interrelationships across both reading and writing. A key concept in the change over time in a successful reader and writer is the strategies which the active, constructor learner comes to apply to problem solving tasks. Reading Recovery assumes that, whatever the origins of their low achievements, less successful readers have to learn to work in the way that successful readers work.*
>
> (Clay, 1992, p. 70)

The Reading Recovery lesson

Each lesson aims to promote this type of problem-solving through engaging the child in several literacy tasks in the daily half-hour lesson. Children in the Reading Recovery Programme have opportunities to:

- discuss and work through understandings of stories
- revise and consolidate known sight vocabulary in a variety of tasks
- develop the four text processing strategies (see Figure 3.3)
- develop reading strategies with texts and apply them immediately when writing
- operate within the alphabetic system through writing and then reading
- segment the sounds within spoken words when both reading and writing
- develop appropriate strategies when reading continuous text to use top-down processing of prediction drawing on context, syntax and background knowledge and then cross-checking through use of bottom-up skills and self-correcting.

This standard format for the lesson also provides the Reading Recovery teacher with rich data for analysing the child's performance in order to monitor progress. There is, therefore, provision for a direct assessment, planning and teaching cycle which allows for the programme to be tailored to individual learning within the suggested tasks.

Reading Recovery is currently available in 28 authorities in the UK with over 1,000 trained Reading Recovery teachers, but this leaves a considerable shortfall if all the children (approximately 10–20 per cent of the school population) at risk of reading failure are to be reached.

What are schools to do at this first stage of intervention?

The demands of the classroom are such that class teachers are unlikely to have time for the intensive, daily half-hour teaching of a 'look-a-like' Reading Recovery Programme. So, which of the various ingredients of the Clay lesson structure are likely to be the most effective and economical of time in terms of results for the child?

In other words, what should the hard-pressed teacher concentrate on and with what approach can she be confident of success? Which aspect of reading should be developed – the top-down or the bottom-up skills? A combination of both? Or either one or the other, depending on the outcome of the individual child's assessment?

Given that we know that children with well-developed phonological skills are very much more likely to be successful at learning to read (see Chapter 3) than those who have not those skills, it is likely that a programme that concentrates on learning letter–sound relationships will be valuable. But will it be sufficient? I have already suggested that the time-honoured remedial programmes that focus on this approach to the exclusion of all else have not had impressive results.

The effectiveness of different class-based programmes

A study by Hatcher, Hulme and Ellis (1994) sheds some light on this issue. The researchers designed a study with 128 Year 2 children experiencing literacy difficulties. They were randomly selected to undergo one of three intervention programmes or to be in a non-intervention control group. The three programmes covered the different theoretical standpoints. The children received additional support in programmes that provided extra help through concentrating on:

- reading alone
- phonological training alone
- reading and phonological training.

The control group received a normal school programme.

The group who were given extra support with both phonological training and their reading made the most progress. Hatcher *et al.* consider that this is due to a phenomenon that they call their 'phonological linkage hypothesis'– that phonological training is only really useful if it is immediately linked to reading. In other words, children who are experiencing difficulty probably cannot make the connection for themselves between the sounds in spoken language and the print on the page when reading and writing, as some children are able to do. These delayed readers are not able to operate within the alphabetic code so they need to be shown explicitly how it works.

Suggestions as to how this can be achieved in the classroom are made by Reason and Boote (1994) in their model, which aims to develop the child's meaning-gaining strategies and abilities in phonics and fluency (fluency is used here to describe the print-processing skills of word recognition) through specifically designed games and tasks. This framework overlays well onto the Adams model (Figure 5.1) of the top-down processing arriving at meaning through the use of context, syntax and semantics, having first grasped the concepts about print; and also the bottom-up processing of the mutually reinforcing skills of phonological and orthographic awareness.

IMPLICATIONS FOR PRACTICE

Supporting the early years child with difficulties

The young child may still be at the Pre-level 1 stage of literacy development described in Chapter 3. The assessment of her understanding of concepts about print (see Clay's Observation Survey, 1993) and an assessment of her ability to identify and label the letters of the alphabet by both names and sounds are the starting points.

As with the National Literacy Strategy *Framework for Teaching* (DfEE, 1998), all teaching of literacy begins with text-level work and with the provision of a book that is within the child's capability at 95 per cent accuracy level. This may need to be a simple caption book at the earliest stages of reading schemes. At this precarious stage of literacy development, it is important that the child reads the whole book for the reward of satisfaction and access to the whole story. The purpose of reading needs to be reinforced through emphasis on the top-down prediction skills with the use of both global and local context cues (see Chapter 2). The level of the book used with the child is crucial. Children experiencing difficulties must not lose sight of the enjoyment of reading and the book attempted needs to have exactly the right level of challenge, but they should not find more than one word in 15–20 too difficult to read. A text that is harder than that for the child will make it impossible for the child's meaning-making strategies to operate.

Book Bands (Reading Recovery National Network, 1998) is a useful publication here. It indicates the different levels of books from published reading schemes, so that only very gradual increases in text difficulty are introduced to the struggling pupil. (See Chapter 5 for further discussion of the appropriate match of book to child.)

National Curriculum (Pre-Level 1)

Observation of the child reading

This supplementary list (see the teaching suggestions in Chapter 3, pages 60–6) covers some of the understandings indicated by the literacy behaviours that are characteristically displayed by the *delayed* reader still at this stage of development.

- *Literacy behaviour* is displayed by the child by:
  - voluntarily choosing and enjoying books
  - reconstructing of the story through both acting like a reader and being able to retell the narrative in the accurate sequence
  - being able to concentrate and focus on the activity for a reasonable time span.
- *Understanding of the literacy task* is demonstrated by:
  - knowing that print has a communicative function
  - being aware of and making use of environmental print, i.e. recognises name tags, labels, notices, messages
  - knowing the conventions of print namely:
    the correct orientation of book – the front and back
    that the illustrations and text tell the story in different but complementary ways
    where you start reading, even when it is not the typical left-hand corner of page
    knowing where the text flows even if it is not the typical sweep back on line
    where to start on the following page
    matching spoken word with printed word.

Teaching approaches to support the child delayed at NC Pre-level 1

The appropriate match of book to child enables the teacher to work with the child by, firstly, undertaking a book introduction before reading and then by encouraging the child to:

- talk about the story
- talk about the illustrations
- guess what might happen in the story

and then re-tell the story from the pictures.

- *Sound awareness* (phonological awareness) is developed by:
  - playing games orally with rhyming words, starting with words that rhyme in the book just read
  - playing games with pictures of rhyming pairs (see the commercially produced-version in Reason and Boote, 1994, p. 101 onwards)

- learning and chanting well-known nursery rhymes, playing with the rhyming words substituting ones that don't rhyme or different ones that do.
- *Print awareness* (orthographic awareness) is developed by:
  - identifying individual distinctive words in the book
  - matching words with word cards
  - matching letters by sight with letter cards (special note should be made of children who have difficulty distinguishing between letters that have similar shapes, for example, p/b/d, m/n, f/t, g/q, h/n, r/n, w/m, v/w)
  - consolidation of letter knowledge through identification with both names and sounds
  - playing games to learn the recommended NLS high-frequency words (DfEE, 1998, p. 60) in the book
  - re-arranging word cards into simple sentences.

Additional teaching note:
Handwriting practice develops formation of letter shapes and reinforces letter–sound association. Also note that it is at this stage that print and sound awareness become more strongly linked and mutually reinforcing.

National Curriculum Level 1 (Early Stage)

Observation of the child reading
The following list of literacy behaviours that demonstrate understanding and progress are characteristically displayed by the child at this delayed stage of literacy development.

- *Literacy behaviour* is displayed by:
  - being able to read text from the previous day with support
  - pointing accurately word-by-word as she/he or adult reads, i.e. with one-to-one correspondence of word to unit of sound.
- *Understanding of the literacy task* is demonstrated by:
  - demonstrating more advanced awareness of concepts of print, namely:
    awareness of punctuation
    knowing the difference between capital and lower-case letters
    reading accurately reversable words, for example, 'was'/'saw'
    knowing the terms 'letter' and 'word'
  - being able to discuss the story plot at a literal level
  - beginning to appreciate that long words when spoken will require a correspondingly long symbol when written, i.e. noticing that it must be 'bicycle' not 'bike'.

- *Print-processing skills* of the child are demonstrated by:
  - accurate knowledge of the alphabet
  - recognising a few high-frequency words out of context
  - having acquired a small sight vocabulary linked to her interests/the reading scheme, and knows all the Reception Year NLS *Framework for Teaching* high-frequency words (DfEE, 1998, p. 60).

Teaching approaches to support the child delayed at NC Level 1 (Early Stage)

Children at this stage are moving from the emergent literacy phase towards the beginning of conventional reading. This means that they are just beginning to get to grips with the alphabetic system. Word skills teaching needs to be developed from the context of the child's reading book, with practice and consolidation from the previous day's book taking place at the beginning of each session. Work continues to build prediction skills using the meaning to inform the problem-solving. Ask questions such as 'What do you think is going to happen?' Different types of text with different formats and patterns of language should be used to familiarise the child with several literary models.

- *Sound awareness* (phonological awareness) can be additionally supported by:
  - reading and writing single letter sounds
  - choosing appropriate words from the text and asking the child to supply words that rhyme, for example, 'mill' – 'hill', 'fill', 'pill', 'kill', 'till', 'chill'. Write them for the child asking her to spell the word for you as she begins to recognise the pattern and understand the task
  - generating other rhyming games from the book read by the child – choose a sentence and invent a rhyming couplet for it, for example, 'The boy can see his Mum' → 'His Mum will pat his tum'. The more nonsensical the greater fun the child will have!
  - encouraging the child to play 'I spy', which is the ability to separate onset and rime
  - practising reading vowel-consonant (V-C) words, for example, 'it', 'at', 'on', 'in'
  - practising reading C-V-C words, for example, 'man', 'sun', 'rat', 'pot', 'pit'
  - helping the child hear the syllables in words beginning with children's names, for example, say 'Can you listen carefully, I am going to say some people's names in bits. Clap once for each bit of the word – Ben-jam-in, Jen-ny, Da-vid, etc.

- *Print awareness* (orthographic awareness, now word recognition) is supported by helping children to:
  - make books on the same theme as the book read, perhaps personalised using the child's name as the main character
  - choose words that extend her sight vocabulary from the book, and take words from the NLS high-frequency words. The child should learn to read and write them.

National Curriculum Level 1 (Later stage)

Observation of the child reading

This list is of literacy behaviours demonstrating understanding and progress which are characteristically displayed by the child at this delayed stage of literacy development.

- *Progress in literacy* is displayed by:
  - greater fluency due to increasing sight vocabulary and improving word-building strategies
  - starting to show awareness of mismatch by self-correcting, plus evidence of scanning ahead
  - spelling becoming more conventional when writing, using invented spelling with her own text.
- *Understanding of the literacy task* is demonstrated by:
  - being able to use all the four cueing systems – *context* (including picture cue), *syntax*, and the *look of the word*, i.e. length/distinctive features, *phonic analysis* (see Figure 3.2). The use of the strategies will be erratic with over-reliance on first one then another cue, but nevertheless the awareness of the different aspects of print is developing
  - beginning to consider the plot and character of the story in greater detail.
- *Print-processing skills* of the child are demonstrated by having an increasing sight word vocabulary (approximately 50 words of the NLS *Framework for Teaching* high-frequency words).

Teaching approaches to support the child delayed at NC Level 1 (Later Stage)

Use the activities as appropriate for the earlier stages. The child will have moved from the logographic phase through to the alphabetic phase of print-processing and will have both strategies at her disposal for reading and writing.

- *Progress in literacy* is demonstrated by:
  - increasing awareness of mismatch and self-corrects
  - reading ahead to problem-solve when not able to read a word
  - being able to see 'little words' in 'big words'

- occasionally being able to analyse whole letter strings and not just decode letter-by-letter (i.e. moving towards the phase of orthographic print processing)
- using an increasingly expressive reading voice.

Use a range of books with child varying vocabulary, language structures and patterns, focus on enjoyment and humour. Following reading discussion about the book, its meaning and any subtleties should continue to reinforce the purpose and satisfaction in reading. Give praise where positive strategies occurred in other words. Make explicit what the child knows and can do with text.

- *Sound awareness* (phonological awareness) is supported by:
  - making explicit the grapheme–phoneme association when reading and writing
  - encouraging the child to read and write words with consonant blends, for example, '*tr*uck', '*sl*im', '*gr*ass'
  - encouraging the child to read and write words with consonant digraphs, for example, '*sh*op', '*ch*ip', '*thr*ush'
  - using knowledge of initial sounds to act as a cue to make a choice between two or three words when reading connected text
  - using analogy to help write new words from known ones, for example, t-*ook* from l-*ook*.
- *Print awareness* (orthographic awareness/word recognition) is developed by:
  - practising sight vocabulary with games, context sentence cards (both commercial and teacher-made), with and without pictures, whole stories
  - using correct spellings of a few common words in the course of her own writing. These will be words within the child's sight vocabulary. When constructing her own text, attention can be drawn to the standard spelling (of one or two words only) with word lists in the classroom or personal word banks when appropriate and in context
  - continuing to learn high-frequency words in the NLS *Framework for Teaching* list (DfEE, 1998, p. 61).

Children still causing concern after this type of additional support and differentiated teaching within the early years classroom will require further discussion with the Special Educational Needs Co-ordinator, and probably need assessment from an outside agency such as the School Psychological Service, following which decisions will be made regarding the appropriate action to be taken.

Summary   This chapter has discussed the fact that learning difficulties are often multi-factorial and that the effect of each additional factor multiplies in impact more and more adversely on the child's functioning. Early diagnosis is important as literacy difficulties become entrenched very quickly, slowing the child's learning and affecting her self-esteem. There are many kinds of intervention for children with literacy difficulties and three of these are addressed, along with the theoretical rationale. The last part of the chapter makes suggestions for an individual programme for the child who has begun to slip behind her classmates. It is based on in-depth assessment of the reader's literacy development and the implementation of customised support for effective literacy learning.

The key points that this chapter has addressed are:

- **the multi-faceted nature of learning difficulty**

- **different types of intervention for delayed readers**

- **suggestions of ways to support a delayed reader in the classroom.**

Further reading

Clay, M.M. (1993) *An Observation Survey of Early Literacy Achievement*, Hong Kong: Heinemann
A useful book for every early years teacher, it describes fully the whole range of literacy assessments for children experiencing difficulties.

Reason, R. and Boote, R. (1994) *Helping Children with Reading and Spelling*, London: Routledge
This book is full of ideas and practical examples to support all children, not only those experiencing difficulty, with their reading and spelling.

The bilingual child in the early years classroom 7

Objectives

When you have read this chapter, you should:

- be aware of the main policy issues regarding the education of bilingual pupils

- understand the theoretical issues concerning the teaching of literacy to bilingual pupils

- understand the ways in which the fluency of bilingual pupils' spoken English can be supported within the classroom

- be able to plan a programme to teach reading for children who are still in the process of acquiring fluency in English.

Introduction

If the language environment is natural, consistent and stimulating, children will pick up whatever languages are around.

(Crystal, 1987)

This book, with its focus on the teaching of reading, needs to consider how to implement a literacy programme not only for mother-tongue English-speaking children, but also the significant number for whom English is an additional language. Given the close links between oracy and literacy, it is essential to discuss the ways that learning to speak English can be supported in the classroom in order to address, in a comprehensive way, the teaching of reading and writing to young bilingual and multilingual pupils. Teachers also need to be aware of the wider context and educational policies within which schools operate. This chapter is aimed, mainly, at enabling teachers to support those children who are still in the early stages of spoken English development.

THE CONTEXT IN THE UK

In an age where travel is becoming ever easier and communications even more rapid, society is correspondingly and increasingly more mobile. The situation in the late 1990s in the UK, as in the rest of Europe, is that a substantial minority of the population is **bilingual** and **multilingual**. Although the figure nationally is around 7 per cent, in some areas of the country, London and Bradford for instance, it is a great deal higher. There are schools in which 90 per cent of the pupils have English as an additional language.

Many multilingual and bilingual citizens in the UK speak English as an additional language, at varying levels of proficiency. In addition, many of them are biliterate. This linguistic and cultural diversity is reflected in our primary schools and is accurately and well described when it is said that there are many young pupils who 'live in two languages' (Hall, 1959).

Teachers are likely to encounter children in this situation at some point in their careers and, when they do, they will need to approach the teaching of literacy from a position of informed professional knowledge and understanding. The UK, as a nation with a population that is bilingual and multilingual, is certainly not unique. Gregory states that:

> a large majority of countries in the world are multilingual. Between four and five thousand languages are spoken in fewer than two hundred states; in Nigeria over five hundred languages are spoken natively, while India claims over sixteen hundred mother tongues. In some countries, literacies in several languages and scripts will stand side-by-side in different types of schools.

(Gregory, 1996, p. 3)

Different countries have different attitudes and policies regarding the education of their bilingual pupils which reflects a variety of situations and contexts. Included in this are issues regarding the balance between and the status of the different languages spoken. Those countries which have two official languages in operation, as in Canada, are more likely to have well organised and carefully thought-out **immersion language programmes** for their emerging bilingual children. In such countries, and Wales and Catalonia are also examples, there is a clear expectation that children will learn to read and write in both official languages. Speakers of other languages arriving in Welsh or Canadian classrooms benefit from the expertise, the level of awareness about bilingualism and the support available.

bilingual
literally, two languages; infers that the individual has a considerable level of competence in the languages

multilingual
literally, many languages; infers that the individual has a considerable level of competence in the languages

immersion language programme
a programme that has the clear expectation that the children will be able to speak, read and write in both languages

This is not the general situation in the UK. The policies, and historically there have been several, result in very varied provision. British primary teachers are aware that schools are required to provide opportunities within appropriate programmes so that the abilities of their bilingual pupils are developed in all aspects of English. It is not only their entitlement, but a necessity. English is the main medium of learning throughout the school; and, crucially, without fluency in English, individuals have difficulty securing social and political rights. But what might be an appropriate programme?

Policies and attitudes to bilingualism in the UK

The response to the flow of immigrants into the UK that occurred in the 1950s and 1960s was the generation of assimilationist policies that aimed to absorb the new entrants as speedily as possible into the language and culture of the UK. This standpoint is reflected in the official documents of the time (for example, the Plowden Report, HMSO, 1967) which made a somewhat pejorative distinction between individuals who have chosen to learn an additional language, with the subsequent intellectual gains and advantages, and the bilingualism of immigrant children, when the second language is learned in a **diglossic situation**. This is where the children are required to learn a higher status language whilst having a first language that has lower status. These bilingual learners are frequently poor, with working-class and linguistically 'disadvantaged' parents.

The model of educational programme that these pupils underwent can be described as one of **submersion** in the new language with a **subtractive type of bilingualism**. The features of this type of programme described by Skutnabb-Kangas (1984) are as follows.

- All curriculum teaching is through the second language, English.
- The acquisition of the second language puts at risk the **mother tongue** which is frequently a low-status minority language.
- The teachers are most commonly monolingual.
- Compensatory, auxiliary teaching of English takes place usually outside the classroom.
- Children are frequently separated and stigmatised for inadequate knowledge of English.
- Parents become passive and negative to the programme due to their own language difficulties.
- Low expectation of the pupils is common.
- The self-esteem of the bilingual learners is low.
- These pupils often experience conflicts of identity, rootlessness and alienation.

diglossic situation
the use of two or more varieties of language (one 'high' or standard variety and one a 'low' or spoken vernacular) for different purposes in the same community

submersion programme
a type of programme that both makes no acknowledgement of the first language; all the teaching is through the second language

subtractive type of bilingualism
Is one that the acquisition of the second language puts at risk the mother tongue which is frequently a low status minority language

mother tongue
the first language of an individual, literally the language learned from one's mother

The Bullock Report (HMSO, 1975) marked a change in attitude in the official position. There was a move away from thinking in terms of separation and compensation, towards the inclusion of bilingual pupils into a society that acknowledged itself to be multicultural and multilingual. The following often quoted and eloquent paragraph depicts this view clearly:

> *No child should be expected to cast off the language and culture of the home as he crosses the school threshold, nor to live and act as though school and home represent two totally separate and different cultures which have to be kept firmly apart. The curriculum should reflect many elements of that part of his life which the child lives outside school.*

(HMSO, 1975, para. 20.5)

The type of educational programme that emerged following such changed thinking upheld the strong belief in the maintenance of the first language as well as recognition of and respect for the culture and the home life. The predominant features (again adapted from Skutnabb-Kangas, 1984) of this type of programme are:

- the emphasis towards functional bilingualism
- the first language is given status by the curriculum being taught through its medium
- no separation of the bilingual group for teaching and consequent stigmatisation for inadequate knowledge of English
- parents are commonly active and involved with these programmes
- English teaching taking place with the whole class
- teacher expectations are high, reflecting the positive stance of the programme, as is the bilingual pupils' self-esteem and self-confidence
- the programme leads to a positive bilingual, bicultural identity.

BILINGUAL PUPILS

As has been discussed, many children in our schools speak English and at least one other language and possibly, in addition, the dialect form of the first language also. Arabic, Bengali, Cantonese, French, Greek, Gujerati, Hindi, Italian, Panjabi, Spanish, Sylheti, Turkish, Twi, Urdu, Welsh and Yoruba are only some of the first languages of the children in UK schools. Some schools have a number of pupils who share the same home language, other schools have children who have many different languages as their mother tongue. Patently, the task for the school in the latter case is very much more complex, in terms of resources and teaching practice.

There are differences between bilingual children in several ways. First, some may be British-born and have experience of English spoken at home but are exposed to varying levels of competence. Secondly, some children may have recently arrived in the UK and within this group there will be disparate levels of receptiveness and motivation to speak and learn English, depending on the circumstances surrounding their entry into the country. The contrast between the traumatic experience of a refugee and the child of a European business man working in the UK will affect greatly the two pupils' predisposition to learn English.

Supporting spoken language development in English

The National Curriculum Orders for English (DfE, 1995) state unequivocally the expectation that all pupils in England will operate within the four modes of spoken and written language, namely, speaking and listening, reading and writing in the English language. Emphasis is placed not only on fluency in English, but also on pupils' need to have access to the use of Standard English when the situation demands it. Bilingual pupils have exemption from the National Curriculum Tasks and Tests for only their first six months after entry to the country. Primary teachers then have the responsibility to ensure that all their pupils are supported and able to fulfil these requirements.

The situation is different in Wales, where Welsh is the official language alongside English. In this case, children who have Welsh as their first language are not expected to follow the Key Stage 1 Programme of Study for English nor be involved in its assessment arrangements.

The principles that underpin any teaching approach which is designed to enable bilingual pupils to acquire fluency in English as an additional language will have much in common with the discussion in Chapter 1 considering the language development in English first language speakers. The main principles in the development of oracy that were addressed are as follows.

- Children learn to speak because they want to communicate in order to fulfil a personal purpose.
- Communication begins with the positive relationship between the communicators. This maybe initially through eye contact alone and later with eye contact and other body language in support of the verbal interaction.
- Learning to speak an additional language in the early years of school develops through stages that mirror the way that the first language was learnt. Children progress typically through the following stages:

- a silent, receptive stage, i.e. understanding but not able to produce language
- one-word stage
- two-word stage
- the over-generalisation of rules, for example, 'peoples'
- the development of vocabulary and the more sophisticated use of connectives.

For children who are already literate in their first language, the processes will be different. Vocabulary and, perhaps, the understanding of the grammatical structures will be acquired through learning to read in the second language as well as through learning to speak.

- Great depth of meaning can be communicated in the one- and two-word stages of language development through the use of body language and intonation.
- The context-bound, concrete-experience-based and highly personal features of communication need to be appreciated and capitalised upon by the more experienced language user.
- The role of the interested adult signalling enjoyment and providing elaborated models of the correct form of the utterance is crucial.
- Written language, in the form of stories, rhymes and poetry, promotes spoken language by offering rich linguistic models for the child.

However, there are important distinctive features in the acquisition of an additional language that need to be recognised. These are as follows.

- The child will already be aware implicitly of the way that languages are structured and work.
- The first language should be the foundation upon which the additional language is grafted in that the child should be acknowledged to be a competent language user already. This underlines the importance of first language maintenance and support.
- Learning a second or additional language enhances cognitive development and linguistic awareness which is especially valuable when the child is learning to read and write.
- Attitudinal aspects to the learning of English contribute a large part to the effectiveness of the teaching approach. The children who feel that their first language, their parents and their culture are respected and drawn upon in school will feel more secure, confident and motivated to speak, read and write English and also to learn through English.

The Australian Ministry of Education (1987, cited by Clarke, 1992) lists specific understandings and technical and refined skills that need to be acquired before a second language can be mastered. These are:

- a new set of sounds and sound groupings, which may or may not be like those of the first language
- new intonation patterns and their meanings and new patterns of stress and pause
- a new script or alphabet (possibly)
- a new set of sound–symbol relationships
- new vocabulary
- new ways of putting words together (a new grammar) and organising information and communication
- new non-verbal signals, and new meanings for old non-verbal signals
- new social signals and new ways of getting things done through language
- new rules about appropriateness of language for specific situations and roles
- new sets of culturally-specific knowledge, values and behaviour
- a new culturally-specific view of the world
- an ability to relate to people and to express feelings and emotions in the new language.

For the young emerging bilingual child, the challenge to acquire fluency in the language of the dominant culture is one of high risk and one that is linked intrinsically with her own cultural identity and with her self-esteem. Awareness of these sensitivities needs to be uppermost in the consciousness of the teacher as she plans her learning environment and programme of work.

IMPLICATIONS FOR PRACTICE

Good practice in the early years classroom

Given the principles discussed, how might they be translated into effective practice? It is only possible for the early years teacher to offer a supportive learning environment, with enriching and purposeful language opportunities for the bilingual pupils if the class is operating within a primary school that has a considered policy and a positive ethos towards the whole of its school community.

School admission policies

On admission the following details can usefully be recorded:

- the languages spoken by the child and in the home
- the level of fluency in both the first language and English

- whether the child is literate in a language other than English
- whether the child has other experiences of school
- whether the child has formal language experiences other than school, for example, learning Hebrew at the synagogue
- the level of fluency of the parents and whether an interpreter will need to be present at parent/teacher discussions
- the religion of the child
- whether there are any special dietary requirements.

Involving parents in the education of bilingual children

If schools are to involve parents in the education of their children, it requires a great deal of energy and effort on the part of the teachers. If they seek to involve the parents of children for whom English is an additional language, it takes genuine understanding and empathy. Teachers need insight into the cultural expectation of the community they serve. Whilst deeply committed to their child's academic success, frequently it is not in the experience of those from other cultures, particularly those from Asian countries, to participate actively in their child's education and school.

On the practical side, parents will only be whole-hearted about involving themselves in their children's education if information about and documentation from the school and its activities are available in the relevant home languages. With this as a starting point, parents will feel welcomed and valued, and in their turn, they will be willing to translate stories, rhymes, notices and labels.

Often adults in the community are able to promote the wider cultural life of their children through teaching all pupils traditional dances, cooking special dishes, celebrating religious festivals, as well as the usual primary school practices of telling stories and supporting art and design and literacy activities. Early years education begins with the whole child and integrates all learning with life both in and out of school. Good relationships with parents are the key to this, and all the pupils, not just those who have English as an additional language, will benefit from celebrating the rich, cultural diversity in the school.

The plurality of the school

Making overt the multicultural nature of the school is the responsibility of all the staff and requires attention to detail and sensitivity towards individuals from other cultures. Resources should approprately reflect the languages and ethnicity of the children in a particular school in interesting and lively ways. Printed material in the form of displays, notices and signs needs to embrace the languages spoken, and all the visual images used need to portray the many cultural influences of the school community. Alphabet and number charts not only demonstrate powerfully the symbolism of arbitrary signs that represent letters and numbers in different systems but also they emphasise the inclusive nature of the school environment. Books, games, jigsaws, and all equipment should depict positive images of ethnic minority people. Cultural artefacts of the relevant countries of origin of the pupils can transform (and transport!) the atmosphere of the home corner and role-play areas. Art materials, wax and pencil crayons need to supplied in colours that allow as realistic a representation as possible of the variations of skin tone. Dolls also should typically represent different races. If measures of this kind are taken, important and positive messages will be sent so that the language and culture of the majority of the population is not seen as repressively dominant within the micro-society of the school.

Bilingual learners along with all pupils need a secure and accepting environment in which to practise and perfect their spoken language.

Stages of learning an additional language

It goes almost without saying that a teacher is only be able to provide appropriate learning activities to enable children to develop their English, if she is clear about the stage of spoken language development of each of the children in her class. Hester's (1990) stages are helpful here, see Figure 7.1.

When teaching children English as an additional language who are at different stages of learning, it should be recognised that fluency in basic interpersonal communicative skills occurs usually after about two years of immersion in the second language. However, it has been suggested that the ability to learn concepts not already established, for example mathematical or scientific concepts, takes much longer (Cummins, 1979). This he calls **cognitive, academic language proficiency**, which appears to take five years or so of immersion in the new language. Interestingly it remains about this length of time whatever the age of the child when she starts to learn the additional language.

Home languages will be viewed positively if children who share the same first language are grouped together for some tasks and if the more experienced speakers are used as interpreters.

All the teacher-led speaking and listening activities such as 'show and tell' can be especially valuable for the bilingual learners in the group if skilfully exploited. Awareness of the ways that they can be used to develop confidence gives a feeling of inclusion and also allows useful practice of a speech structure which some of the class are finding difficult.

cognitive, academic language proficiency
the ability to learn concepts not already established, for example mathematical or scientific concepts in a second language

Figure 7.1
Stages of English learning

The following scale describes aspects of bilingual children's development through English which teachers might find helpful. It is important to remember that children may move into English in very individual ways, and that the experience for an older child will be different from that of a young child. The scales emphasise the social aspects of learning, as well as the linguistic. Obviously attitudes in the school to children and the languages they speak will influence their confidence in using both their first and second languages.

Stage 1: *new to English*
Makes contact with another child in the class. Joins in activities with other children, but may not speak. Uses non-verbal gestures to indicate meaning – particularly needs, likes and dislikes. Watches carefully what other children are doing, and often imitates them. Listens carefully and often 'echoes' words and phrases of other children and adults. Needs opportunities for listening to the sounds, rhythms and tunes of English through songs, rhymes, stories and conversations. If young may join in repeating refrain of a story. Beginning to label objects in the classroom, and personal things. Beginning to put words together into holistic phrases (e.g. no come here, where find it, no eating that). May be involved in classroom learning activities in the first language with children who speak the same first language. May choose to use first language only in most contexts. May be willing to write in the first language (if s/he can), and if invited to. May be reticent with unknown adults. May be very aware of negative attitudes by peer group to the first language. May choose to move into English through story and reading, rather than speaking.

Stage 2: *becoming familiar with English*
Growing confidence in using the English s/he is acquiring. Growing ability to move between the languages, and to hold conversations in English with peer groups. Simple holistic phrases may be combined or expanded to communicate new ideas. Beginning to sort out small details (e.g. 'he' and 'she' distinction) but more interested in communicating meaning than in 'correctness'. Increasing control of the English tense system in particular contexts, such as story-telling, reporting events and activities that s/he has been involved in, and from book language. Understands more English

than s/he can use. Growing vocabulary for naming objects and events, and beginning to describe in more detail (e.g. colour, size, quantity) and use simple adverbs. Increasingly confident in taking part in activities with other children through English. Beginning to write simple stories, often modelled on those s/he has heard read aloud. Beginning to write simple accounts of activities she has been involved in, but may need support from adults and other child, her/his first language if s/he needs to. Continuing to rely on support of her friends.

Stage 3: *becoming confident as a user of English*
Shows great confidence in using English in most social situations. This confidence may mask the need for support in taking on other registers (e.g. in science investigation, in historical research). Growing command of the grammatical system of English – including complex verbal meanings (relationships of time, expressing tentativeness and subtle intention with might, could, etc.) and more complex sentence structure. Developing an understanding of metaphor and pun. Pronunciation may be very native-speaker like, especially that of young children. Widening vocabulary from reading a story, poems and information books and from being involved in maths and science investigations, and other curriculum areas. May choose to explore complex ideas (e.g. in drama/role play) in the first language with children who share the same first language.

Stage 4: *a very fluent user of English in most social and learning contexts*
A very experienced user of English, and exceptionally fluent in many contexts. May continue to need support in understanding subtle nuances of metaphor, and in Anglo-centric cultural content in poems and literature. Confident in exchanges and collaboration with English-speaking peers. Writing confidently in English with a growing competence over different genre. Continuing and new development in English drawn from own reading and books read aloud. New developments often revealed in own writing. Will move with ease between English and the first language depending on the contexts s/he finds herself in, what s/he judges appropriate, and the encouragement of the school.

(Hester, 1990, p. 41)

CASE STUDY

Supporting language development

The class is discussing how to make a dolls' house. Every child is invited to make a contribution to the topic and is encouraged to use the sentence constructions 'My dolls' house will be made of. . . I will use. . . This is because. . .'

In what other ways is the teacher able to utilise traditional early years approaches and group teaching methods to support the developing spoken language of all the pupils?

Teachers need to introduce tasks to bilingual pupils with concrete examples to aid better understanding of what is to be done. An introduction to an art and design project or a science task is best done alongside the materials in the specific area, with a demonstration of the activity as an example of what is expected, immediately before it is to be carried out, thus reinforcing expectations of involvement.

Reporting back in a plenary session needs to be similarly embedded in the context and accompanied by the painting, model or print with a clear and simple explanation of how it was made. Bilingual learners will gradually be able to report back on their own work if given appropriate support (either by a friend or an adult) when giving the report and with possibly a prior rehearsal of what and how it is to be said. Games of the turn-taking and of the sentence-completion type can be useful for learning vocabulary and also for practising particular structures, for example, 'I went to the shop to buy a brand new. . .*a*lligator/*B*eano Annual/*c*alendar/*d*inosaur/*e*lephant. . .' The list could be usefully scribed by the adult with the letters of the alphabet written and emphasised in another colour.

Children teaching children

Practically-based experiences are important for all early years pupils, but for emerging bilinguals they are essential. Children learning an additional language need contextual and visual support for any educational task they engage with. In addition, working alongside fluent English speakers provides both with opportunities to interact with valuable spoken language role models. Games and structured play provision offer stress-free and sufficiently open-ended learning for children to put their developing skills to good use.

The role-play area is particularly rich in both learning opportunities for the children and observation opportunities for the teacher.

CASE STUDY

Spoken language development through play

Simon (5 years) and David (4 years) are playing in the home corner. Simon says to Abdul (5 years):

'Abdul, you play with us, you play with us.
(To children outside) You can't come in.
Abdul's playing here. You can't come in, Abdul's playing here.
Abdul do you want a dress?
Would you like a dress?
Do you want a dress?
Do you want a dress?
Do you want a nice dress, Abdul?
Here is a dress, Abdul.
This is gorgeous Abdul.
Good boy Abdul.
That is gorgeous, Abdul.'

Simon holds up a voluminous flowing skirt. He says:

'Put your feet in, Abdul.
Put your feet in, Abdul.
This is gorgeous, Abdul.
Put your feet in, Abdul.'

Simon tries to push Abdul into the skirt.

Abdul: 'No'
Simon: 'Abdul, you are a good boy.
          Abdul, you're a good boy.
          Abdul is a good boy in the home corner.'

1 What in particular does Simon intuitively do to enable Abdul to understand him?
2 List four different ways of capturing attention and reinforcing meaning.
3 How does it differ from an exchange that Abdul might have with an adult in the class?

Whilst one might not applaud the coercion on this bilingual child newly arrived in a reception class, it cannot be denied that this conversational exchange is facilitative for Abdul's spoken English.

Children learn successfully through interaction with and learning alongside their peers. Sociable and compatible pupils from the same class demonstrate that they are able to support intuitively the language development of their friends. Both the patient repetition and the contextually-embedded nature of the situation play a powerful part in the reasons that make the learning so effective. Collaborative language games, either made by the teacher or commercially-produced, of the board and playing card type, promote vocabulary practice, as do problem-solving tasks in design and technology, science and construction activities.

Learning language through stories

Every early years teacher will be quick to exploit the use of high-quality stories in her classroom to develop the oracy for all the children, both monolingual and those for whom English is an additional language. Hester (1983) has made helpful suggestions as to how this might be achieved. The following list is compiled from hers:

- using a story board to retell a favourite well-known story
- making and then labelling models arising from the story
- collections of items that can be used in the retelling (or reworking through imaginative play) of a story, for example, dolls' house chairs, bowls, beds of different sizes and a doll in order to retell *Goldilocks and the Three Bears*. These are known in some parts of the country as 'story boxes'. The mini collections are stored in labelled boxes for ease of storage and access
- retelling and sequencing a story through a set of pictures drawn either by the child herself or photocopied from the book
- bingo games of the words used in a simple book
- making a concept 'map' of a story
- making simple 2-D flannel puppets and using a 'fuzzy felt' board to retell the story
- making a dual-text version of the story with the help of a parent or more experienced speaker of the first language
- writing a new ending or different beginning of the story
- following up an aspect of the story – researching about elephants, the countries they come from, drawing them, making a frieze, doing the drama, etc. after reading *Tusk, Tusk* (McKee, 1978).

Learning to read and write in English

It has been stated that the learning of literacy has its foundation in rich and meaningful opportunity to use spoken language. You will recall, also, that the literacy process is one that is multi-faceted and inter-related (see the series introduction and Chapter 5). For bilingual children learning to read in English this holds true, but some of the aspects of the process will be more useful and accessible than others.

A bilingual child's processing of text

Chapters 2 and 3 discussed the differing roles of the top-down and bottom-up processors that operate when reading text to inform the individual about the written words. When reading, writers such as Adams and Clay propose that the top-down aspect relies on the context. This includes both the global context (meaning of the overall story) and also the semantic and syntactic context (the internal sense and grammar of the sentence) which enable the reader to predict what a word is likely to be. These predictions are then confirmed (or not!) by the bottom-up processing which involves a grasp of the grapheme–phoneme associations of the word or, put another way, the awareness of the alphabetic code. If pupils are reading in their mother tongue, and if they have had appropriate teaching, both of these two processing strategies are likely to be used equally. In fact, Adams and Clay would say that they both need to be drawn upon, in parallel and simultaneously, and that fluent, fast reading depends upon the ability to do that.

The bilingual child, however, due to her relatively weaker knowledge of the language structures of English has less familiarity with its patterns, vocabulary, sentence structure and grammar, and so finds this ability to predict text more difficult. It is likely that the bilingual novice reader will find the bottom-up processing of text more useful and hence she relies heavily on her decoding strategies.

She will almost certainly have an appreciation of the one-to-oneness of spoken units of sound to print. This will depend in part whether she is functional in another script and whether this prior knowledge is from an alphabetic or logographic script. Also Sassoon (1995) points out that pupils familiar with much more complex scripts (such as Chinese or Japanese which place huge demands on the visual memory) will find the orthography of the English language relatively straightforward and so will be advantaged. However, there is a risk that if all the focus is on the decoding aspect of reading, the comprehension and an appreciation of the meaning of text will be lost.

CASE STUDY

Playing with language in a text

Gregory (1996) demonstrates this beautifully with her transcript of the young bilingual child at the early literacy stage (National Curriculum Pre-level 1) of acting like a reader with one of the Mr Men books, *Mr Bump* by Roger Hargreaves.

continued...

'Kalchuma: (turning the pages and 'reading' each word very definitely) Bump.
              Mr Bump is go to gone bump.
              Mr Bump is go to gone.
              Mr Bump is to all down.
              He went there to bump.
              Mr Bump to. . .what's in there missing?
              Mr Bump go stick. . .his stick, there stick. (means a sticking plaster)
(continues using similar English constructions "go to go/go sitting/go he go to his steps, etc." throughout a number of books).'

(Gregory, 1996, p. 57)

1 Which kinds of books are particularly supportive of the young bilingual child's early attempts at reading?
2 Which books will encourage an appreciation of the language patterns and structures of English?

Bilingual children are aware of the code aspect of written language. This is possibly because they have experience of literacy in another language, even if they are not fully biliterate, or because they are older and more experienced about print when they operate in the early stages of reading in English in school. This is demonstrated well by Kalchuma's use of strategies. It is clear that she has an idea of the one-to-oneness of a word representing a unit of sound. She has a developing print awareness and a small sight vocabulary which is shown by the way that she uses letter shapes to inform her 'reading' and 'Mr Bump' is recognised and said, as is 'go' and the beginning 'st. . .' of sticking plaster. Much harder for this child is prediction through remembering accurately the pattern and rhythm of the written language, although clearly this book has been read and re-read often. This is the aspect that a mother tongue reader would find the easiest, as shown in the story of the 5-year-old saying to her teacher about a well known and much loved book "Look miss, I can read so good now I can even do it with me eyes closed'!

'Inside-out' approach to teaching reading

This approach to teaching children to read in a language that is not the mother tongue is described in detail by Gregory (1996) and is essentially 'starting from the known'. As she says:

> The child's cultural knowledge is used rather as a spring board for comparing differences and similarities between languages and cultural practices, for showing children that stepping into a new world

provides access to exciting experiences but need not mean abandoning the language and culture of home.

(Gregory, 1996, p. 101)

In this important way Gregory sees the teacher as a mediator. Language learning through activities such as cooking and socio-dramatic play are good for linking the familiar with the new. Making foods that have equivalents in different countries, such as breads or soups, and learning the words for them in the languages, can be followed by stories and rhymes about food. This type of work capitalises on what is a daily experience and compares it with and relates it to the novel.

Children at this stage of learning to read, whilst still learning to speak English fluently, need to become familiar with a bank of words and phrases in English. Gregory calls these 'chunks of language'. The fact that the words and groups of words will be specific to that situation and that book is not important, as over time and given many opportunities the words and phrases will mesh together and so provide a deep understanding of the patterns and rythms of English. The use of verse and rhymes both orally and in reading is of great value to the child at this stage, as the rhyme is a mnemonic for remembering the exact way the words are placed together. 'Chunks' are needed if syntactic prediction (of 'what sort of word is likely to fit here?') cueing systems are to kick in and so become a useful reading strategy.

Learning 'chunks of language' occurs most naturally in a situation that is embedded in a practical context. Frequently, adults learn a second language in the context of restaurants and travel situations and so memorise accurately whole coversations in order to reserve tables when hungry and to buy tickets for flights when needing to return home. In the same way, children will learn through the doing of activities in order to get them done. Reading and writing goes alongside this, with one language mode supporting the use of the other. As we have seen earlier, with the monolingual child the book made of the class activity embeds the activity in the permanent evidence of the class book to be shared and enjoyed. The visit to the pond is followed by the jointly illustrated and written book. Sentences and parts of sentences are used, rehearsed, sounded out and written down and then read back. Gregory extends this approach for teaching bilingual children to read through enabling the prior learning of 'chunks' of language and practice of the structures of language soon to be encountered in a story, perhaps through the use of puppets or drama activities before reading the book. This is an elaboration of Clay's rich book introduction described in

Chapter 3. Gregory uses this technique to go one step beyond, raising expectation of what language structures might be to the actual rehearsal of structures and words. This enhances the child's ability to utilise prediction as a cueing strategy even if initially it is through partially memorised text.

Words and phrases are learned through the support of written language in the manner of *Breakthrough to Literacy* (Mackay *et al.*, 1970), with look-a-like materials where keywords are written on strips of card, which then are read, made into sentences, re-arranged and read again, and learned. Re-reading on subsequent days makes the spoken and written language links internalised through practice and familiarity.

'Outside-in' approach to teaching reading

Gregory (1996) writes about the 'outside-in' approach as being complementary to the previous one and as a means of 'introducing the unknown' and this she bases on the work of Meek (1981). This way into reading capitalises on the magic of stories to internalise literary conventions, vocabulary and experiences beyond their world. Through this process, children learn the 'grammar' of stories as Harold Rosen (1985) says stories are 'the commonest possession of humankind – part of the deep stucture of the grammar of the world'.

Stories that are memorable and contain layers of meaning (discussed fully in Chapter 8) have the richest potential for language learning. Gregory demonstrates how the traditional tale of *The Little Red Hen* can provide the opportunity for the child to come to at least four different types of understanding:

- semantic knowledge, or understanding about the world and its practices, such as in the case of this book – flour is made from grain and bread is made from flour, etc.
- syntactic knowledge, or 'chunks of language', with the repeated phrases of 'Who will help me?', 'No I won't'
- lexical knowledge, or words that form meaning (lexical) sets, such as 'cut'/'corn', 'plant'/'seeds', 'bake'/'cake', 'mill'/'grind'
- orthographic/grapho-phonic knowledge, such as b-*ake*/c-*ake*/r-*ake*.

How stories are read and discussed is crucial in order to capitalise on the utmost potential of the book. This is explored in more depth in Chapter 8. The NLS *Framework for Teaching* endorses this way of working with texts, with the approach of shared reading (see Chapter 2). This approach allows for groups of children to have opportunies to learn spoken language and to practise reading together with mutual support. Hard-pressed teachers will maximise the learning through group approaches, to develop the spoken and written language of the bilingual children in their classes alongside their monolingual peers. A sound understanding of both the theoretical issues and the learning needs of each child in her class will mean that it is more likely that the teacher is able to offer the appropriate provision for her bilingual pupils.

Summary

This chapter has discussed the major theoretical issues concerning the teaching of literacy to bilingual pupils, so that you are aware of the main policy issues regarding the education of bilingual pupils. You should now understand how the fluency of bilingual pupils' spoken English can be supported within the classroom and also be able to plan a programme to teach reading to children who are still in the process of acquiring English fluency.

The key points that have been addressed in this chapter are that:

- **various countries implement different types of programme to support bilingual learners**

- **children for whom English is an additional language bring particular strengths and understandings to the task of literacy.**

Further reading

Siraj-Blatchford, I. (1995) *The Early Years: Laying the Foundations for Racial Equality,* Stoke-on-Trent: Trentham Books
A readable overview of the important issues that need to underpin the thinking and practice of every early years teacher.

Gregory, E. (1996) *Making Sense of a New World,* London: Paul Chapman Publishing
An informed and detailed account of young children's literacy learning in a second language. Compulsory reading for anyone teaching in a school with pupils for whom English is an additional language.

Children's books and the early years classroom 8

When you have read this chapter, you should:

- understand the reasons why books are a rich and flexible resource for the teaching of literacy

- be knowledgeable about children's literature and its potential to promote intellectual, emotional and moral development

- be aware of the different types of non-fiction text and how to use information books with pupils

- know the criteria for choosing books for the classroom.

... language written down is thereby cut loose. . .or disembedded. . . from the context of on-going activities and feelings in which speech functions and on which speech thrives. Once on the page, language is on its own. *This gives it a degree of independence which makes it particularly apt for the development of certain kinds of thought.*

(Donaldson, 1993, p. 50)

It is essential that a book focusing on the development and teaching of reading should include a section on the value and use of children's books. Books are both the mainstay of, and the chief purpose for, learning to read. They provide the main source of motivation for galvanising effort when learning to read. Books are *the* most valuable resource for the teacher in the early years of education, offering as they do the potential to delight, to inform, to instruct, to enrich, to teach and for pure enjoyment. This chapter aims to cover the use, selection and promotion of both fiction and non-fiction books not only to advance the reading skills of the children but also, crucially, to develop their overall intellectual, emotional, aesthetic and moral growth in particular and important ways.

THE POTENTIAL OF BOOKS TO DEVELOP LANGUAGE

Books provide the most enjoyable and accessible means of offering children good models of expression that enhance their own spoken and written language. This potential to support language acquisition is a very important one (see Chapter 1). It is through language that we become truly human and separate from animals. Through language, we are able to escape the immediate and are provided with the tools to make sense of the present and to plan for the future (Tucker, 1993). Books present children with the arresting and continually reinforcing manifestation of the differences between written and spoken language (Chapter 3). The experience of books enhances the child's vocabulary, understanding of written sentence structure and the cohesion of text. Through exposure to high quality books children are introduced to a literary language, its conventions and its structures. Tucker continues with:

> *Good writing for this age group from a literary point of view should be fresh, direct and rhythmic – easy to remember and a pleasure to listen to. Short, spare sentences are preferable to long rambling structures, and a bright, lively vocabulary better than a dull repetitive one.*

(Tucker, 1993, p. 117)

Books should provide a pleasurable vehicle for the child to experience and to read flowing, rhythmic language – language that is attractive to the ear when read aloud. On the nature of the language used there has been great debate regarding the benefit of a natural language style and its ability to facilitate comprehension and reading development in young readers. Many texts used with novice readers capitalise on the familiar spoken language patterns of the pupils, but Perrera (1993) suggests that 'a more judicious blend of familiar and more literary grammatical structures will be just the right combination' (p. 96) for some more knowledgeable and advanced readers. The writing conventions in the genre of non-fiction texts can present particular difficulties for young readers, as will be discussed later.

THE PLACE OF WRITTEN LANGUAGE IN DEVELOPING THOUGHT

Books, it has been suggested, provide the most accesssible models of written language to which the child has exposure. If spoken language releases the individual from the 'here and now' (Tucker, 1993), Donaldson argues that the power of written language is that by its 'disembeddedness' it has the potential to develop in the child the ability to think in the abstract as the quote at the beginning of this chapter explains. She continues:

> *I have in mind thought that is about general topics with no imme-*
> *diate bearing on the personal life. For instance, how do birds find*
> *their way when they migrate? Or why does concrete set so hard?*

(Donaldson, 1993, p. 50)

Donaldson suggests that whilst the desire to understand precedes and exists without literacy, it is greatly promoted by access to written language. This is achieved in two ways, firstly by the individual having the opportunity and recourse to sources beyond her experience, namely, to look up information in books. Secondly, literacy promotes the ability to sustain and to order thought. Frequently, this is achieved through writing down one's thoughts and systematically redrafting and ordering them. In this way, 'Thinking itself draws great strength from literacy' (1993, p. 50). Books provide models for this type of ordered, systematic thought.

This form of thinking is essential for success in any field of academic study and educational endeavour, as it lays the foundations for being able to follow or structure an argument, for the ability to go beyond the personal and to generalise from the evidence provided. Impersonal, disembedded thought, and then its linguistic expression, is part of the cultural heritage of every pupil and her educational entitlement: it is the key to success in the educational system and an advanced society depends upon it.

FICTION: CONCERNING NARRATIVE

The role of literature in the development of the child

The literary critics of children's books have for many years been aware of the power of stories to affect the child's development for good or for ill. The statement that literature can influence strongly the perceptions and opinions of the individual is one that needs no support from research evidence. All of us can remember vividly the effect of a particular novel on our emotions, on our views and on understandings. In my teens I read avidly historical novels, those of D.K. Broster (sadly now out of print), Margaret Irwin, Rosemary Sutcliff and Alison Uttley. I can still recall the excitement, terror and passion they evoked as I voraciously read far into the night about battles on windswept Scottish moors, the beheading of queens, and the privations of Roman Britain. I can remember not only the feelings and pleasures evoked by my reading but also the circumstance and place where I was when I read the books. I can still feel my arm numb with cold through reading in bed and holding a novel for hours outside the bedcovers in a unheated bedroom, the sound of the big band music on my brother's gramophone in the next bedroom, the smell of the library book pages and the taste of the Crunchie bar that frequently accompanied the reading – a synaesthesia of experience. In my imagination I was literally lost in the lives of the book characters for days, much to the exasperation of my family.

Books and moral development

The powerful effect of reading on one's imagination can also be a potentially damaging effect on the morals of susceptible adolescents. The influence of books on moral development was taken so seriously in the 1950s and 1960s that my convent school had a list of novels which we were forbidden and even the reading of them was considered a venial sin. All the novels by D.H. Lawrence were predictable targets, but some of the books turned out to be a huge disappointment and for which it was certainly not worth jeopardising one's immortal soul or still worse incurring the wrath of Reverend Mother! The reason for the Catholic Church's disapproval in these instances still remains a mystery. Needless to say, the list of 'banned' books probably did more to promote reading than any of the suggestions I will make later in this chapter!

The issue for the teacher today is how to select the books that are worth using with pupils – books that have the potential to 'move children on', to promote understanding as well as to enthrall. Tucker (1993) quotes from Walter de la Mare, 'Only the rarest kind of best in anything can be good enough for the young' (1941, p. 11), in order to reinforce the responsibility invested in adults to make judicious decisions regarding the books in their classrooms. As a psychologist Tucker argues, an important developmental task for the child is to be able to escape 'from egocentricity in favour of a world view that can take into account attitudes and knowledge other than one's own' (1993, p. 118).

'Good' and 'light' books

Books can undoubtedly be instrumental in enabling the individual to take on another's point of view and is perhaps one of the essential criteria that should be applied. It is this feature, Tucker suggests, that separates a 'good' book from a 'light' one. He says good books:

> *succeed in going beyond mere story telling towards sharing a particularly interesting or relevant individual vision of the world with the reader. By the end of the story. . .readers may well feel that*

they have somehow advanced in their own understanding, not just of the book but of some of the rest of life as well.

(Tucker, 1993, p. 118)

Whilst he admits that this definition of 'good' is simplistic, Tucker considers nevertheless, that it is a helpful distinction for the teacher to make. The criterion of a 'good' book is one that addresses serious topics in a readable and enjoyable way. It is not that the book is 'heavy' or overtly didactic or moralising, but that it has layers of meaning beyond the basic story line. The book in the opposite category, the 'light' book in Tucker's terms, is one that does not attempt to challenge nor to address the uncomfortable and is more likely to offer stereotypes and social prejudices and clear-cut distinctions of good and evil in its safe, predictable, albeit often addictive stories. Both types of book contribute to the diet of readers of all ages, but the latter may not have sufficient potential to reward use with children in school. Books used in an educational setting need to offer satisfaction and the potential for discussion. To Tucker's classification of 'good' and 'light' (and the distinction is not absolute), I would add 'great' books (and perhaps these are the classics). Such literature would represent the ultimate on the continuum of the categorisation. 'Great' books stand the test of time, they have within them the power to transport, to enchant and to alter an individual for ever. A 'great' book lives on in the memory and fuels the imagination. Such a book with these dimensions is Alice Holm's (1965) classic, *I am David*.

I am David is the story of a young boy, perhaps 10 or 11 years old, who has lived all his life in an internment camp somewhere in central Europe. In the prison camp he has been educated by a cultured man, taught to speak several languages and endowed with a philosophy of life that transcends the miserable, brutalising existence of the camp. David escapes with the help of a guard and begins his archetypal journey from the country in which he has been imprisoned, through Italy and up to Denmark in the search of a woman whose address and photograph he has been given. On the way he has many encounters and adventures.

This beautiful book raises the eternal questions that surround human existence – issues of right and wrong, freedom and imprisonment, birth and death, hope and despair, joy and suffering, endurance, faith and, ultimately, loss and gain. This type of literary experience offers opportunity to learn more about the world, a kind of 'felt history'. Also, through engaging with *I am David*, the child is able to learn more about herself and others, and to try to make sense of the enduring values in life.

Not all 'great' and 'good' books, of course, are so ambitious in the issues they tackle, nor are they so profound or painful. Neither is *I am David* a book for an early years class. But other classics provide glimpses of some of these mind-broadening and enhancing topics. *Not Now Bernard* by David McKee (1980) operates at several levels. At one level, Bernard desperately and unsuccessfully attempts to attract and hold the attention of his parents. This book achieves great humour despite the polite cruelty of the aloof, detached adults. McKee has several 'big' themes in *Not Now Bernard*. With reflection and through discussion, children will become aware of, perhaps, the 'monster' in us all that needs to be at least acknowledged. Maybe the readers will pick up on the way that families operate, the power that adults have over children and the power children can also exert over adults. Either or both of these interpretations (or indeed others) are valid.

The complexity deepens further because, whatever the book, its type and its content will only influence an individual who is in a psychological and intellectual position to be receptive. So with good books, not only are several interpretations possible but different readers will 'see' and are able to 'see' only certain meanings to a story depending on the experiences they bring to it.

Reader response
When reading a text (and what might constitute a text will be explored later) a child brings to it highly individual, preconceived notions of the world, shaped by previous experience. This personal state of mind and being fundamentally affects what meaning is extracted from a book. Expanding on the cause of the variations of reader reponse, Evans (1998) says:

> *All children have different societal, and cultural backgrounds and all, at the end of the twentieth century are now 'caught' by many hybridised worlds: the world of television, the world of advertising, computers. . .the ever changing social rules and values required by today's youth culture. . .*

(Evans, 1998, p. xiii)

This predisposition affects the meaning the reader is able to attribute to a text. Evans continues:

> *Factors such as race, gender and social class all have a part to play in forming our previous experiences and therefore influencing the way in which we are able to make sense out of texts.*

(Evans, 1998, p. xiv)

Conversely, it is those books which have the most potential to influence the individual that present the widest range of possibilities for interpretation. The more multi-faceted, the greater the number of layers of meaning, the more the book draws on previous experience and understanding of the world, the wider the range of possible understandings there are. As Anthony Browne says:

> *I deliberately make my books so that they are open to different interpretations, most of which I never hear about (probably just as well). Once a book is finished I have to let it go, like a child. What happens next is out of my control.*

(Browne, 1998, p. 195, cited by Evans, 1998, p. xvi)

Browne's statement draws on the ideas of Rosenblatt (1938), presented in her seminal work on reader response which goes so far as to say, about the relationship between text and reader, that no text exists until it is read or 'interpreted' by an individual. The black marks on the page only come alive when read and this reader will possess a set of ideas, prior knowledge and a socio-cultural heritage. Figure 8.1 helps to demonstrate this inter-relationship.

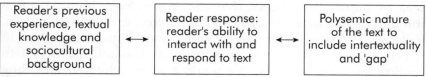

Figure 8.1
The relationship between the reader and the text

(Rosenblatt, 1938, cited by Evans, 1998, p. xv)

As hinted at earlier, young readers can be supported to be more penetrating and perceptive of the layers of insight held in a text. This does *not* mean a cold dissection of every story shared with a group of 4-year-olds, but more the teacher's encouragement to exploit the relationship of reader and text in a way that is personally meaningful. Pupils need to be given, firstly, the opportunity to enjoy 'good' and even 'great' books, and then to explore them through discussion and allow each person individual time to think and respond.

Types of fiction book

Picture books

The elevation of the picture book into a category of literature of its own has occurred over the last two decades and has been described significantly by Beard (1987) as the 'Third Golden Age' of children's literature. The importance of the picture book as a significant separate genre in its own right has been recognised by critics and much has been written on the topic which is well summarised by Egoff (1981):

> *The picture book, which appears to be the cosiest and most gentle of genres, actually produces the greatest social and aesthetic tensions in the field of children's literature.*

(cited by Evans, 1998, p. xiii)

The reason for this due recognition of the stature of the picture book is that it is an art form in its own right, bridging the worlds of art and design and literature. Much of the exploration of the issues concerning these beautiful, intriguing and hugely complex books I will have to leave to others in dedicated volumes, such as those of Styles and Watson (1996) and Evans (1998). However, a précis of the main ideas of the discussion will be attempted in order to proceed with the argument about the value of picture books as a crucial resource in the early years classroom.

The picture book as a polysemic text

Modern life has brought enormous change, creating flux in every area of human life. These changes to our lives, brought about through the advances in medicine, technology and communication, have altered irretrievably the economy, society and the culture in which we live. Those of us born half-way through the twentieth century can only guess at the world that the children attending nursery school today will experience during their lifetime. These pre-schoolers, in the words of the poet, Kahil Gibran, 'dwell in the house of tomorrow'.

These changes, and the challenges that they bring, have altered the way in which texts are viewed and made sense of. Texts have increasingly come to include the visual, dance, drama, music, media and information and communications technology, in addition to more traditional written texts. A sign system (semiotic) perspective broadens 'a text' to cover any 'chunk of meaning' (Short, 1986) which, perhaps surprisingly, includes mathematics, movement or a mime. A recent cartoon typified this new feature of life today with a picture of a teacher giving a puzzled child a book with the exhortation 'Take it – you will enjoy it – it's a bit like a CD-ROM!'

Inevitably this broadening of the categories of what constitutes a text also widens the meaning of what it is to 'read'. Kress and van Leeuwen (1996) and Kress (1997) explore the inclusive term of visual literacies to embrace the notion of the 'reading' of illustrations, diagrams, computer logos and graphics and maps, as well as paintings and sculptures. This broader definition of reading is touched upon in Chapter 2. Picture books demand such 'reading' as they are far, far more complex than a book with pictures depicting a story. The format of the book, the setting of the print and the illustrations on the pages and the interdependence of the illustration with the text are all integral to the whole. They are important features of the way that the story is told. The 'reading' of these 'signs' is crucial to the meaning making of the 'text' as a whole.

The children's author Anthony Browne states:

> Making *a picture book, for me, is not like writing a story then painting some pictures. . .No, it is more like planning a film, where each page is a scene that includes both words and images inextricably linked. What excites me. . .is working out the rhythm of the story and seeing how much is told by the pictures, how much by the words, and how much by the gap between the two.*

(cited in Evans, 1998, p. 198)

The elegant simplicity of many of the examples of good picture books belie the complexity behind their conception, which needs thoughtful 'unpacking' by a well-informed adult with small groups of children, if the book's richness and depth is to be realised.

The concept of the narrative picture book is the telling of a story, often layering it with deeper meaning through the technique of **intertextuality**. Intertextuality capitalises on reference to traditional tales and other well-known stories with which it is assumed the child is familiar and able to draw on. The prime examples of the use of intertext are the Jolly Postman books by Allan and Janet Ahlberg (1986, 1988, 1991 and 1995). These delightful and supremely skilful books intrigue and amuse children of all ages from nursery to the end of primary school, and are capable of being appreciated at different levels. They are, however, rendered completely incomprehensible to children for whom English is an additional language or newly arrived in the UK and for whom the English traditional tales and nursery rhymes are not part of their cultural heritage.

intertextuality
implicit references within a text to other texts, without recognition of which the reader will not gain as much meaning as she might otherwise do

Other examples of intertextuality are the books, with longer text, of Robert Munsch and Babette Cole who overturn the telling of fairy tales with a fond tongue-in-cheek look at the sexist image they frequently portray. Munsch's *The Paper Bag Princess* and Cole's *Prince Cinders* and *Princess Smarty Pants* gently parody the much-loved tales and in so doing raise awareness of gender and equality issues in the young audience. Justifiably, picture books are described as

polysemic
having multiple levels of meaning, in ways that do not allow any final, fixed meaning to be pinned down

complex, with as great an aesthetic appeal as they are **polysemic** and open to multiple interpretation.

Books without words and longer texts

Wordless books present the emerging reader with opportunities and challenges. A book with no printed text has a universal appeal, as clearly it can be used with all primary school pupils and with all stages of English as an additional language. Visual images have the immense advantage that they convey meaning in a way that needs no linguistic interpretation. These books are designed using multiple and very detailed pictures, each depicting a time frame of a single action in the unfolding of the story. The size of the frames controls the pace and the dramatic intensity of the action. Raymond Briggs immediately comes to mind as, perhaps, the most renowned illustrator/author of this type of picture book. Many thousands of young pupils have developed their story-telling skills, and reinforced left-to-right directional sense and, in addition, simply delighted in 'reading' the myriad of beautifully drawn pictures in his classic, *The Snowman* (1978) and the Father Christmas books. Although the latter are a hybrid between wordless books and comic/cartoon books, as they contain the occasional thought or speech bubble.

This type of book, it has been argued, is pleasurable only for those children with an already well-developed narrative ability, as many are left feeling insecure and longing for words to complete the visual story-telling (Graham, 1998). It would appear that the transformation from visual to verbal is more difficult than assumed for many pupils. It also appears that wordless books are both too painstaking and perhaps rather unappealing to make, as many talented picture book author/illustrators have no titles of wordless books against their names.

Books with a greater amount of more complex written text also have their place in the early years classroom and certainly by Year 2. They will need to be read to a group in serial style or probably will require adult support in a shared reading situation.

The use of picture books as a way into print

The intricately crafted picture book is a powerful tool for learning in that it provides children with the opportunity to become aware of art and design issues. In other words, pupils in the nursery, reception and years 1 and 2 are enticed into becoming visually literate. This genre of children's literature helps novice readers into making sense of the print through the appealing format and supportive illustrations. Through repeated and enjoyable encounters with picture books, both alongside an experienced reader and

independently, children in the emergent stage of literacy development are enabled to progress to the beginning of conventional
reading (see Chapter 4).

The different ways picture books support early reading

Before children are ready to read print, picture books are a prime
source of learning about the nature and purpose of reading, in both
the broader and more traditional senses. The illustrations not only
give the books appeal, accessibility and interest for those at this
very early stage of literacy, but they also provide a cueing system
for those in the transitional stage, as children are motivated and
supported to move towards beginning reading conventionally (see
Chapter 4). Children for whom English is an additional language
are assisted by the visual element which is integral to the text and
as such facilitates interpretation of the meaning. In an interesting
project, using ethnographic research methodology, Parkes (1998)
studied very young pre-schoolers working with picture books. The
study sheds further light on the processes involved before conventional decoding can occur and conventional reading take place
(again see Chapter 4.). Parkes found that each time the text was
read and re-read the child interacted with the text in different and
increasingly more sophisticated ways. She says:

> As children became more familiar with the books and as their
> experiential and linguistic facility increased, so too did their
> interactions. They noticed similarities within and across books;
> made text to life and life to text connections; and borrowed some of
> the language of books to use for their own purposes. In short, the
> books became a lived-in and lived-through experience. A further
> finding was recognition of the active role children assumed as
> meaning makers.
>
> (Parkes, 1998, p. 45)

Wells (1987) also noted that children of this age who had opportunity to become immersed in 'good' books played more imaginatively
and for longer periods of time, mirroring the anecdotal experience
cited of the older reader of the potent effect of novels on understanding and imagination.

The last sentence of the Parkes' quotation echos an often repeated
assertion in earlier chapters in this volume about the impressive
capacity of the child to make meaning. With a picture book the
emergent reader, after hearing the text from an experienced literacy
user, is able to 'read' all the signs on the page (i.e. illustrations,
format, placing of the print) to reconstruct for herself a narrative
that is personally significant and that makes sense. The intricate

detail of the illustrations are 'read' and interpreted to construct the child's story. Layered texts such as John Burningham's (1977) *Come Away From The Water, Shirley!*, with the double-page spread pictures depicting Shirley's imaginative fantasies alongside the everyday stuff of living, are recognised for what they are and woven into the child's telling, so demonstrating remarkable insights. As they revisit a favourite text, children make multiple interpretations by continuing to appreciate further features, one detail assuming prominence at one time and then another quite different emphasis at a further telling. About this finding Parkes writes:

> The text and illustration form an open potential, part of a semiotic data pool, through which the child constantly generates new hypotheses and discovers new meanings. As young children return to previously read books in collaborative and independent reading situations they are able to draw on and make use of the sign systems which are meaningful to them.
>
> (Parkes, 1998, p. 50)

This experience provides the emergent reader with the precurser to the later development of the top-down processing needed for the decoding of print (see the series introduction and Chapter 2). A skilled adult sharing a picture book with a small group, or using the large text version with a larger group of young pupils, helps to develop and then reinforce the prerequisite understandings of concepts about print (see Chapter 4). Later in the reception class and Year 1, picture books will be used to form the basis of systematic direct teaching of print and sound awareness, and perhaps also wider cross-curricular or topic work will emanate from the engagement of the class with a much enjoyed shared story (see Chapter 5) capitalised upon for several learning purposes.

Further implications for practice

Early years educators will be aware that in order for their pupils to become avid, competent readers, they themselves have to be enthusiastic and informed about children's literature. Books for the whole school and those for each class have to be selected carefully according to rigorous and appropriate criteria.

The choice of books for the school

The considerations to be addressed when compiling book collections are:

- to maintain a balanced, attractive range of high-quality children's literature
- to meet the learning needs, abilities and interests of the pupils

- to ensure that all the books are appealing and in good condition
- to have any portrayal of a culture, race or gender represented fairly and without bias
- to aim to purchase stock regularly so that the library and class-room collections remain fresh, up-to-date, topical and tempting.

Book areas should reflect these considerations. They should be well thought-out, comfortable and meticulously cared for. The up-keep of a book area needs to be one of the priorities in all early years settings and should be seen as an integral part of the learning environment. Books need to be changed frequently to reflect current interests or a theme and to encourage the spending of time in the area and browsing. It is the book area that sends one of the most potent messages regarding the extent to which books are valued by those who work in the classroom.

Encounters with books in nursery and school should be carefully planned and designed to delight the children, to motivate them into reading the book and to deepen their understanding of the story and, even, an aspect of life itself.

Reading stories to children

Storytime is the prime example of just such an experience. Through reading stories, the adult has a valuable and regular opportunity to promote interest in books and demonstrate her enthusiasm in stories. In consequence, storytime requires careful planning. The timing needs to be thought about, usually stories are read at the end of sessions, but variation can be useful to generate fresh stimulation, so to start a session with a story or to revisit the previous day's book can be very effective.

Introducing the book

The value of breaking the ground before reading the book is now well known (Clay, 1991) and the benefit of the teacher preparing the pupils with a rich introduction is acknowledged. This 'tuning in' will include looking at and discussing the cover, title and author; exploring what the children think the content might be about, the 'big' ideas and the characters; appreciating and 'reading' the illustrations, looking at the illustrator's style and approach to the construction of the format, if the book in question is a picture book; making links with books previously enjoyed, explaining words that might not be understood.

All adults working with very young pupils will appreciate the importance of everyone being quiet, settled and listening before the story is begun. Are all the children comfortable, do they have sufficient space and are they able to see the pictures?

Reading the story

The reading of the story itself requires thought and practice. Story tapes are excellent models for the inexperienced to become aware of the effect of intonation, pace and dramatic pauses. With rehearsal, the use of different voices, facial expressions and gesture can all contribute to enhancing the experience to make it truly spell binding.

Discussion

The follow-up discussion and questioning is an important aspect of storytime and as such needs to be planned. Here I am addressing the wider issues connected with the book as literature rather than a lesson to teach an aspect of reading development; this is addressed fully in Chapter 5. Whenever the story is shared sufficient time should be allowed for discussion, savouring of the illustrations and certain aspects of the narrative.

How a book can be enjoyed after story reading

After storytime, the book should be left to be looked at or re-read in the book area. If the story reading has been taped, that too can be left to enhance later enjoyment. Occasionally stories can be followed up with the children writing and illustrating their own or alternative versions of the story.

All encounters with children's literature should aim to encourage the pupil's response to the text through expression of thoughts and feelings about the story, to develop critical awareness and to deepen understanding and enjoyment of books.

NON-FICTION BOOKS: READING TO LEARN

The term 'non-fiction' as it is used here to describe all books that are not story books is an over-simplification in the extreme. Several authors have argued that the terms 'information' or 'reference' books are unsatisfactory also, based as they are on a definition of content. None of these terms do justice to the complexity of the range of meanings and linguistic forms of this important category of books (Littlefair, 1993). However, for the purpose of convenience in this section of this chapter regarding the use of information texts in the early years classroom, I shall adopt the generic term 'non-fiction' to cover the books under discussion.

Rationale for the use of non-fiction texts

There are several reasons why this chapter includes a section about the importance of deepening and enhancing children's responses to non-fiction texts.

- Firstly, school and university learning is largely dependent upon the development of appropriate study skills and the ability to use reference books and other sources of written information. We have discussed earlier in this chapter that Donaldson believes non-fiction books have an important role in facilitating abstract thought, that is, thinking in an impersonal and disembedded way.
- Secondly, the bulk of adult experience of interacting with text is with non-fiction texts. There are many adults who rarely read novels at all but who rely heavily on information books in order to function at work and at home.
- Thirdly, there is disturbing evidence that indicates that boys lag behind girls in English (particularly reading and writing) from as early as the end of Key Stage 1 and, all through Key Stage 2 and 3, up to GCSE. The quango then called the School's Curriculum and Assessment Authority (SCAA, 1995) has suggested that perhaps with greater emphasis and more informed support in the primary school, boys could be motivated, stimulated and challenged into wider reading. This will include greater use of non-fiction books. This is an issue that we cannot afford to ignore in the early years of education.

Teachers need to be both knowledgeable and actively enthusiastic about the promotion and use of lively, attractive non-fiction texts, so that all children are able to read effectively to obtain information. Learning to read and reading to learn are both crucial tasks of the primary school.

What evidence is there that there is a problem?

It is not a new concern that primary-aged children are unable to use non-fiction texts appropriately. HMI reported in 1991 that it would seem that teachers are much more secure in their understandings about how to develop children's reading and writing in fiction than they are with non-fiction. This difficulty that children demonstrate with their comprehension of and inability to use non-fiction texts appropriately is demonstrated through their writing. The Exeter study (EXEL) has focused on this area of pupils' literacy and Wray and Lewis (1997) identify the all too common 'copying out' phenomenon as the most obvious symptom indicating difficulty. This is despite exhortation from the School's Examination and Assessment Council Report (SEAC, 1991, p. 19) which states that 'Pupils should be given opportunities to "reshape" information, into a form different from its source and always for a communicative purpose.' This clearly presents young children with a challenge. In order to achieve the task of 'reshaping' information, pupils have to enter, as discussed earlier, into the realm of familiarity with

Donaldson's (1993) 'language of systematic thought'. This clearly has defeated many children and also, it would appear, their teachers' ability to support them to develop this skill.

How can pupils be best supported?

Research evidence in Australia (Littlefair, 1991) has suggested that only a greater attention to the children's awareness of genre in both their reading and writing will enable teachers to help their pupils to cope with the literacy demands of school and beyond.

Comprehension goes beyond decoding the words. In order to access the sense, children have to be aware of the way that different types of meaning are commonly expressed in our culture. The most common expression of meaning that children meet in school and at home is narrative. Children listen to narrative in conversations and in stories that are read to them, and they watch and listen to drama-tised tales on television even before learning to read. Children become familiar with the structure of story, the setting, the intro-duction of the characters, the unfolding action, possibly a crisis and then a resolution, which is often a happy ending! The language used, with which they are most familiar, is specific to the narrative genre.

When young readers meet non-fiction texts, they meet quite different forms of meaning, which is reflected in the different structures and form. Halliday (1978) suggests that children need to understand the varieties of language that are used for different purposes and different audiences. Writers choose the appropriate genre for the purpose for the writing. Littlefair suggests that:

> *We know through experience how to organise a letter to a bank manager, a shopping list or an explanation of how to cook a special dish. As soon as we have a purpose for communication we usually know how to organise it.*

(Littlefair, 1993)

This tacit knowledge of form and purpose needs support in order to be developed and extended into more complex writing. In this way, Littlefair argues that genre and purpose are synonymous and that these types of texts fulfil a variety of purposes.

Types of non-fiction text

Narrative non-fiction
Narrative non-fiction includes information stories, biographies and procedural writing. These 'interest' books and information books

are organised chronologically within a time sequence. Examples of this type of book are *My Friend Whale* (James, 1992), which handles facts about whales in an accessible way that mirrors the narrative genre.

This type of non-fiction book lends itself particularly to the early years classroom. The advantage is that it can be more easily read aloud or used in group reading sessions (see Chapter 2). The language adopted is usually more accessible and rhythmic than non-narrative non-fiction books. The disadvantage is that these books cannot, so conveniently, be used easily to retrieve facts, although this can be achieved with thorough **indexing**.

index
a list of names and subjects covered in a book, which indicates also where they can be found

Other examples of non-fiction information stories are diaries and biographies which are less likely to be used with the very youngest pupils, except, perhaps, for the quality and aesthetic appeal of the illustrations. For example, *The Country Diary of an Edwardian Lady* might be made available as part of a science display of plants, flowers and leaves after a class walk in the park.

The type of writing that is organised procedurally includes notices and books of instructions, such as guide books, sets of instructions, manuals, stage directions and forms. The most common form of procedural writing that young pupils encounter in school are recipes used in cookery sessions and the rules and instructions for games. At home, of course, it is a different matter as this is the most common form of non-fiction text. Children observe adults reading instructions before taking medication, before using a new piece of equipment or seeking help from a manual when experiencing trouble with a car, video or computer.

Non-narrative non-fiction
This category of non-fiction book covers the vast majority of what is termed 'reference books' and covers all the following:

- plans, maps, diagrams and computer printouts
- dictionaries, word books, computer data, road signs and logos
- lists of contents, indexes, library classification and library catalogues
- thesauruses, encyclopaedias, subject reference books and databases.

Expositionary texts
Expositionary texts describe, explain and, on occasions present arguments. They frequently contain considerable amounts of text and the style of the written language often places great demands on young readers. The books in this category of text are:

- interest and information books – non-chronological
- newspapers, magazines and advertisements.

Difficulties with expositionary texts

Many young readers who are able to read narrative probably require further support in order to read non-narrative texts. This issue is of great importance to the teachers of the older early years pupils. The literary means by which authors express their intentions is highly sophisticated, and that is before the subject matter and its comprehensibility is considered. As Donaldson says, children:

> *need now to enlarge their understanding of the many ways in which words can be handled with skill on the printed page – handled to achieve economy, or elegance, or emphasis or surprise, or cohesion between sentences, or logical clarity in a sustained argument, to name only a few of the aims that concern an author.*

(Donaldson, 1993, p. 29)

The key to understanding the challenges these texts present is a knowledge of register and genre which provide the linguistic tools with which to evaluate books for primary children. A writer, it has been suggested, chooses a genre appropriate for his or her purpose. The genre form relates to the cultural form of expressing meaning, and can be considered the framework of a written or spoken communication. The writer expresses the details of the communication in a register of language which is inevitably constrained by the immediate situation and its conventions.

Features of registers in expositionary texts

The language of this important non-narrative genre is complex and presents the greatest challenge to young readers. It is the language of exploration, description, of persuasion and argument. In explanations and descriptions the texts are arranged quite differently from narrative. They may be based on a series of facts that offer an explanation. They are non-chronological and the reader is not borne along by the dynamics of a story. There might be a notion of problem and solution, compare and contrast, of cause and effect.

CASE STUDY

An extract from an information text

'By 1600, however, low-lying land like this in the Netherlands has been drained to grow crops. . .They dug huge drainage channels and built windmills to pump water from the land into these channels taking it to the sea. The newly-reclaimed land was used to graze livestock and later ploughed to grow crops.'

(Sauvain, 1995, p. 21)

What could you do as the teacher to enable children to make sense of this as they read it?

The grammar used by writers of expositionary texts is complex. The devices used to link parts of the text may be difficult to follow, and the use of the passive voice adds to this opacity. Longer sentences, with complex introductions, are frequently seen in these books, making great demands on the reader's short-term memory.

There are often a larger number of content words, in which the meaning is 'packed'. Content words may be technical words in subject specific texts. The density of the meaning is due also to the ideas and concepts being discussed.

CASE STUDY

An extract from an information text

'Unlike deciduous trees, conifers do not shed their needles annually. Their needles last two to three years. When they fall from the tree they take a long time to decompose, and the humus they produce is quite acidic.'

(Felts, 1996)

Which technical terms would you discuss with children before using the book in class and how would you tackle the task?

This accessible and attractive 'pop-up' book, produced with the younger reader in mind, needs the adult to work with and explain terminology to the child.

Implications for practice

The role of the adult

Publishers are becoming more sensitive to the difficulties experienced by primary aged children reading non-fiction texts, and much has been achieved in the last few years to improve the accessibility of information books generally. The teacher can be a powerful support, enabling young readers interact with non-fiction literature.

> *Reading to learn what is known must include the habit of freshly wondering; knowledge must be re-constructed by the learner.*

> (Meek, 1991, p. 170)

Children can be encouraged to 'freshly wonder'. This active process of creating meaning from text needs to be understood by teacher and child. Through spoken language the adult is able to demonstrate to the pupil the cognitive strategies that have to occur in order to make sense of the text. In discussion the links between what she knows and what the text is conveying can be achieved. Once again this refers to what Donaldson describes as 'embedding the thinking'. The difficulty arises from the fact that the majority of the thinking required by non-narrative texts is 'disembedded' and is not centred in an immediate or personal context – the phenomena addressed are not in the child's first-hand experience.

The adult is able to help the children first by organising the prior experience 'what do we already know about. . .lighthouses?'. The offering of new learning is made real and meaningful through an activity or a visit. In other words, the learning is made concrete by the first-hand experience and this is often used well by primary teachers, before they turn to secondary sources of books. The teaching sequence is then followed up or 'sealed' with an appropriate story or poem to deepen learning.

Helping children to use information texts

Browne (1997) is very clear that children need to be encouraged to read non-narrative books early and with a clear idea of their function. She says that children in the nursery and reception class:

> *need to understand that they are a resource for learning, that if they want to pursue an interest, explore an idea or discover the answer to a question and an information book may be able to help them.*

> (Browne, 1997)

She continues that the best way to do this is by the adult modelling reading a list of contents, looking and reading quickly through, pointing out text guides such as sideheadings, using the index, giving an overview of the information presented. Adults demonstrate in this way that one book can be rejected in favour of another and that selective reading is valuable use of time.

> *Children become critical readers as they begin to realise that some books do a better job than others.*
>
> (McKenzie and Warlow, 1977, p. 48)

Neate (1992) suggests that infant children need to be shown how to find a book they require for a particular purpose by looking at the:

- cover
- title
- list of contents
- index
- headings and sub-headings

and by:

- scanning the book to locate the appropriate section
- skimming through the pages which contain the relevant information.

Supporting the search for and use of information

Indeed, the teacher will have employed her critical faculties to assess the suitability of the non-fiction book through the evaluation of the quality of these features and their potential to help the child into the meaning of the text.

Wray (1997) suggests from his classroom-based research project (EXEL), that attempted to scaffold children in their use of non-narrative texts, that pupils' ability to use non-fiction books appropriately and effectively to extend their own learning could be powerfully developed. Wray explains this scaffolding strategy as the use of KWL (know, want, learn) grids:

- What do I *know*? (now)
- What do I *want* to find out? (from the text)
- What did I *learn*? (from reading and working with the text).

This strategy is paralleled by the EXEL team's suggestion for the use of complementary writing frames which aim to provide support in structuring a piece of non-narrative text, for example:

- Although I already knew that. . .
- I have learnt some new facts. I have learnt that. . .
- I also learnt that. . .

- Another fact that I learnt. . .
- However, the most interesting thing I learnt was. . .

Roger Beard (at the Leeds University, School of Education, Saturday Seminar Series, May 1997) proposes a less formulaic approach, but does suggest that comprehension skills need to be systematically taught, along with effective modes of information retrieval. The approaches are aimed more at the later years of primary education, but Key Stage 1 teachers might use the approach with very able readers. Beard suggests that children have to be taught the way that texts work and how to skim read in order to locate the key sentence of a paragraph in order to access the meaning. The development of argument can also be followed and used as a model for pupils' own writing.

The criteria for choice of non-fiction books
The following is adapted from Mallett (1992).

There will be overlap obviously between the criteria for the choice of narrative and non-narrative books:

- attractive format, print and layout
- illustrations that integrate well with text
- clear, lively writing
- new words introduced gradually
- words likely to be unfamiliar embedded in context
- efficient, easy-to-use retrieval devices, namely glossary, contents page and index
- books with a chronological sequence, for example, life cycle or life stories especially for younger readers
- clear topic presentation at beginning of book
- good overall organisation (global structure)
- good linkage at sentence level (local cohesion)
- freedom from stereotyping, misrepresenting either gender or ethnic minorities
- factually reliable given current state of knowledge
- not presenting as neutral information and issues which can be seen from different viewpoints
- books that are lively, thought-provoking and that encourage voluntary reading.

WAYS OF GETTING CHILDREN HOOKED ON BOOKS

The following is adapted from Browne (1996).

Encouraging children to read is an essential part of the teaching of reading. In order to promote books, teachers need the knowledge, energy, time, thought and resources, *and* they need all these in abundance. Teachers also have the delightful task of staying abreast of the latest publications so that they can purchase and advise children on their developing reading preferences. The learning and progress of the pupils' reading development literally depends upon it.

Early years educators may want to consider the following suggestions.

- Ensure a variety of fiction and non-fiction books in the library and classroom including poetry, joke books, teacher and child made books and recipe books.
- Display books in an interesting, attractive, clearly organised and accessible way.
- Have books only that are in good condition.
- Change books regularly.
- Maintain comfortable, attractive, inviting reading areas in every classroom.
- Have a good supply of taped stories, commercially- and school-produced, plus spare blank tapes for recording storytimes and child taped stories.
- Books need to span a wide range of interest and reading levels.
- Invite adults, visitors, and older pupils to share books as frequently as possible with children.
- Encourage the sharing of both adults' and pupils' reflections and opinions about books.
- Make class books whenever topic or other work lends itself.
- Guide choice by offering suggestions of books that will match children's interests.
- Have a home–school reading policy which includes good quality books of literature.
- Organise an annual book week.
- Set up a school book club.
- Hold a second-hand book sale once a year – sell only books that are in good condition, advertise well and start collecting early.
- Reinforce the pleasure of using the school library by holding storytimes in it.
- Take children to the public library.
- Introduce new books at circle time or assembly.
- Make displays of new books.
- Begin a book and then encourage children to complete the reading.
- Offer inspection copies of books for children to evaluate.
- Make displays of each chapter of the class book as it is read.

- Organise additional story-telling and story-reading sessions for specific groups of children such as bilingual learners, advanced or slower readers.
- Be alert to a book programme on TV or radio and, perhaps, match a book to its focus.
- Have a 'book of the week' display. After reading it children can add to the display with a review, with a picture or their response.
- Play games based on books, for example, 'I am thinking about a book that has a very naughty baby in it. The baby shakes talcum powder all over the bathroom. Does anyone know which book I am thinking about?'
- Use extracts of books on the computer.
- Capitalise on computer programmes that are based on books.
- Begin and maintain a chart of 'Books we have enjoyed'.
- Have a puppet theatre available for children to dramatise stories and recollect the language of books.
- Seek the advice of the children before purchasing books – 'Which is the best book you have read?'
- Put the children's book reviews inside the back covers of books to encourage others to read, respond and maybe disagree.
- Explicitly enjoy books yourself in the way that you talk about books and reading.

Conclusion

The primary teacher has the most awesome responsibility to motivate, teach, support and encourage her pupils into becoming fully literate by the age of 11 years. The early years teacher begins this endeavour, as the Ministry of Education in New Zealand (1995) says:

> *Reading programmes should be child centred.*
> *Reading for meaning is paramount.*
> *Reading must always be rewarding.*
> *Children learn to read by reading.*
> *Children learn best on books that have meaning and are rewarding.*
> *The best approach to teaching reading is a combination of approaches.*
> *The best cure for reading failure is good first teaching.*
> The foundations of literacy are laid in the early years.

This book has been written to uphold and to exemplify these principles. In addition, I would add, that teachers who understand the complexity of how children learn to read are in a much better position to offer a structured, multi-approach programme that supports all the aspects of print-processing, that is necessary for fluent reading in the first years of school.

This chapter has focused on the huge potential of books in the classroom as a motivation for reading, as a learning resource and as a delight. Books can be used to promote both a love of reading and to teach reading. Non-fiction texts are potentially a source of interest and information, but there is evidence that they can be poorly used in primary schools. The reading skills that children require to capitalise on the opportunities these texts offer, have to be supported by the well informed teacher.

The key points that have been addressed in this chapter are that:

- **teachers who teach literacy are also teachers of literature**

- **both require energy and knowledge in abundance if teaching is to be successful.**

Mallett, M. (1992) *Making Facts Matter: Reading Non-Fiction 5–11*, London: Paul Chapman Publishing
An extremely helpful book on the use of non-fiction in the primary classroom.

Tucker, N. (1981) *The Child and the Book*, Cambridge: Cambridge University Press
This seminal book on the great potential of children's literature should be read by every aspiring primary teacher.

Glossary

alphabetic code	a system of symbols representing the constituent sounds within words, for **encoding** (q.v.) the spoken word and **decoding** (q.v.) the written word
bilingual	literally, two languages; infers that the individual has a considerable level of competence in the languages; see also **multilingual**
bottom-up processing	the aspect of the reading process concerned with identifying the words on the page
closed question	question to which there is only one right answer; tends to ask for information retrieval
cognitive, academic language proficiency	the ability to learn concepts not already established, for example mathematical or scientific concepts in a second language
concepts about print	the concepts that children develop about how print works to represent spoken language, which can be demonstrated by their reading behaviours
cues	the clues a reader uses in identifying words and determining meanings
cultural practice	value-imbued activities and situations characteristic of a cultural or subcultural lifestyle, e.g., the birthday party, the stag night, the dinner party, the bed-time story
data-narrative	diary, coding and recording behaviours of subjects
decoding	the process of identifying the written word using the **alphabetic code** (q.v.) to determine pronunciation and meaning
diglossic situation	the use of two or more varieties of language (one 'high' or standard variety and one a 'low' or spoken vernacular) for different purposes in the same community
dyslexia	literally, difficulty with reading; a complex syndrome in which the child often presents, on a continuum of severity, visual and aural perceptual and sequencing difficulties that appear not to have been caused by inappropriate teaching or to be the result of poor motivation
encoding	the process of representing the spoken word in writing using the symbols of the **alphabetic code** (q.v.)
functional literacy	the level of literacy needed to operate reasonably effectively in a literate society
global context	the 'big picture' – the wider context of the whole story
glue ear	a medical condition in which repeated ear infections have resulted in a build-up of a thick, glue-like liquid in the inner ear
grapheme	the alphabetic representation of a **phoneme** (q.v.), e.g. 'rough' represents the three phonemes /r/+/u/+/ff/
immersion language programme	a programme that has the clear expectation that the children will be able to speak, read and write in both languages

index	a list of names and subjects covered in a book, which indicates also where they can be found
intertextuality	implicit references within a text to other texts, without recognition of which the reader will not gain as much meaning as she might otherwise do
intrasyllabic unit	a unit of onset plus rime within (intra-) a **syllable** (q.v.)
invented spelling	spelling words phonically using emerging print/sound knowledge; enables the child to work within the alphabetic system making explicit to herself and to her teacher what she knows; supports the development of bottom-up processing
lexicon	dictionary or, when used by psychologists, mental dictionary; refers to the memory store for words, their spellings and sounds
local context	the elements that are local to the sentence – the developing meaning and the developing grammar of the sentence
logogen	the mental construct employed by psychologists in discussing the ways words are represented in the mental **lexicon** (q.v.) to permit word recognition
logogram	written symbol that represents a whole word, as in Chinese, or as with the ampersand (&)
logographic phase	the earliest phase of the sight-recognition of words
meta-language	the technical term used to describe the properties of language; terms like 'sentence', 'word' and 'morpheme' are meta-linguistic terms
miscue	an error or mistake in reading a word, resulting from processing or taking into account only a part of the information available
miscue analysis	a verbatim record of a child's reading and analysis of the **miscues** (q.v.) to identify the strategies being used and future needs
mother tongue	the first language of an individual, literally the language learned from one's mother
multilingual	literally, many languages; infers that the individual has a considerable level of competence in the languages; see also **bilingual**
onset	beginning **phoneme** (q.v.) of word/**syllable** (q.v.), precedes the vowel sound (the **rime**, q.v.), e.g., **b**-at or **br**-at
open question	question to which there is more than one answer, or one way of answering; seeks information and at best prompts new thinking
orthographic awareness	the visual equivalent of **phonological awareness** (q.v.); alertness to the spelling sequences that constitute written words, e.g. a child may learn that '-ing' is the common spelling of the endings of a number of different words and is a reliable guide to pronunciation
phoneme	the smallest unit of sound in a word; a phoneme may be represented by one, two, three or four letters, e.g. **t**o, sh**oe**, thr**ough**
phonemic segmentation	the skill of distinguishing the individual phonemes in words, e.g. the four phonemes in 'fox'
phonological awareness	the perceptual alertness to the constituent sounds within words, ranging from alertness to rhymes and alliteration to distinguishing the individual phonemes

polysemic	having multiple levels of meaning, in ways that do not allow any final, fixed meaning to be pinned down
rhyme	words containing the same **rime** in their final **syllable** are said to rhyme, e.g. acrob**at**/ch**at**, d**own**/cl**own**; however, words are said to rhyme also when they have the same *sound* in their final syllable – these are known as *near rhymes* or *aural rhymes*
rime	the vowel sound and any subsequent consonant sounds of a word/**syllable** (q.v.), following the **onset** (q.v.), e.g., b-**at** and br-**at**
running reading record	a quantative and qualitative analysis of the child's reading to identify the progress being made and **cueing** (q.v.) systems being used
scaffold	a metaphor to indicate the external support or cognitive help an adult can give children while they are internally constructing or developing schemas or concepts
semantics	meanings – both the meaning of individual words and the meaning of complete texts
shared reading	where an adult and child(ren) work on a text together, the adult demonstrating and encouraging reading behaviours and skills
shared writing	adult and child(ren) working together on a writing task, eliciting wordings and spellings by appropriate prompts
sight vocabulary	words that an individual can recognise at sight without having to decode
situated dialogue	dialogue that is embedded and given meaning by its context in a shared situation, e.g. 'Don't!'; more widely, dialogue embedded in lifestyle and value systems
subtractive type of bilingualism	Is one that the acquisition of the second language puts at risk the **mother tongue** (q.v.) which is frequently a low status minority language
submersion programme	a type of programme that both makes no acknowledgement of the first language; all the teaching is through the second language
syllable	the phonological unit in a word that centres on a vowel sound, together with its associated consonants
syntax	grammar – the ways that words go together (word order) to make sentences
top-down processing	processing that informs the identification of words from the context by anticipating what the text is likely to say
transactional stance	attitude and approach, preparedness and receptivity

References I

ACADEMIC REFERENCES

Adams, M.J. (1990) *Beginning to Read: Thinking and Learning about Print*, Cambridge, Mass: The MIT Press

Adams, M.J. (1993) 'Beginning to read: An overview', in Beard, R. (ed.) (1993) op. cit.

Aubrey, C. (1993) 'An investigation of the mathematical competencies which young children bring to school', *British Educational Research Journal*, Vol. 19, No. 1, pp 19–27

Baker, P. and Raban, B. (1991) 'Reading before and after the early days of schooling', *Reading*, April, pp 6–13

Beard, R. (1987) *Developing Reading 3–13*, London: Hodder & Stoughton

Beard, R. (1990) *Developing Reading 3–13*, 2nd edition, Sevenoaks: Hodder & Stoughton

Beard, R. (ed.) (1993) *Teaching Literacy Balancing Perspectives*, London: Hodder & Stoughton

Beard, R. (ed.) (1995) *Rhyme, Reading and Writing*, London: Hodder & Stoughton

Bialystok, E. (1991) 'Letters, sounds and symbols: Changes in children's understanding of written language', *Applied Psycholinguistics*, 12, pp 75–89

Bielby, N. (1994) *Making Sense of Reading: The New Phonics and Its Practical Implications*, Leamington Spa: Scholastic Publications Ltd

Bielby, N. (1998) *How to Teach Reading: A Balanced Approach*, Leamington Spa: Scholastic Publications Ltd

Bielby, N. (1999) *Teaching Reading at Key Stage 2*, Cheltenham: Stanley Thornes

Blagg, N. (1981) 'The diagnosis of learning difficulties', in Somerset Education Authority, *Ways and Means 2: Children with Learning Difficulties*, Hong Kong: Globe Education

Blatchford, P. (1991) 'Children writing at 7 years: Associations with handwriting on school entry and pre-school factors', *British Journal of Educational Psychology*, 61, pp 73–84

Blatchford, P., Burke, J., Farquhar, C., Plewis, I. and Tizard, B. (1987) 'Associations between pre-school reading related skills and later reading achievement', *British Educational Research Journal*, Vol. 13, No. 1, pp 15–23

Blatchford, P. and Plewis, I. (1990) 'Pre-school reading related skills and later reading achievement: Further evidence', *British Educational Research Journal*, Vol. 16, No. 4, pp 425–8

Bond, G.L. and Dykstra, R. (1967) 'The co-operative research program in first grade reading instruction', *Reading Research Quarterly*, 2, pp 5–142

Bradley, L. and Bryant, P.E. (1983) 'Categorising sounds and learning to read: A causal connection', *Nature*, 310, pp 419–21

Browne, A. (1996) *Developing Language and Literacy 3–8*, London: Paul Chapman Publishing

Browne, A. (1998) *A Practical Guide to Teaching Reading in the Early Years*, London: Paul Chapman Publishing

Browne, A. (1999) *Teaching Writing at Key Stage 1 and Before*, Cheltenham: Stanley Thornes

Bruce, J. (1964) 'The analysis of word sounds', *British Journal of Educational Psychology*, 34, pp 154–70

Bruner, J. (1966) *Toward a Theory of Instruction*, New York: W.W. Norton

Bryant, P.E. and Bradley, L. (1980) 'Why children sometimes write words which they do not read', in Frith, U. (ed.) (1980) op. cit.

Bryant, P.E. and Bradley, L. (1985) *Children's Reading Problems*, Oxford: Basil Blackwell

Bryant, P.E., Bradley, L., Maclean, M. and Crossland, J. (1989) 'Nursery rhymes, phonological skills and reading', *Journal of Child Language*, 16, pp 407–28

Chall, J.S. (1967) *Learning to Read: The Great Debate*, New York: McGraw-Hill

Chomsky, N.(1957) *Syntactic Structures*, The Hague: Mouton

Clark, M.M. (1976) *Young Fluent Readers*, London: Heinemann Educational Books

Clarke, P. (1992) *English as a Second Language in Early Childhood*, Multicultural Resource Centre, Australia

Clay, M.M. (1972) *The Early Detection of Reading Difficulties: A Diagnostic Survey with Recovery Procedures*, Portsmouth: Heinemann (3rd edition, 1985)

Clay, M.M. (1979) *Reading: The Patterning of Complex Behaviour*, London: Heinemann Educational Books (new edition, 1985)

Clay, M.M. (1987) 'Implementing reading recovery: Systematic adaptations to an education innovation', *New Zealand Journal of Education Studies*, Vol. 22, No. 1

Clay, M.M. (1991) *Becoming Literate: The Construction of Inner Control*, London: Heinemann

Clay, M.M. (1992) 'A second chance to learn literacy', in Cline, T. (ed.) (1992) *The Assessment of Special Educational Needs*, London and New York: Routledge

Clay, M.M. (1993) *An Observational Survey of Early Literacy Achievement*, Hong Kong: Heinemann

Clay, M.M. and Cazden, C.B. (1990) 'A Vygotskian interpretation of reading recovery', in Moll, L.C. (ed.) (1990) op. cit.

Crevola, C.A. and Hill, P.W. (1998) 'Evaluation of a whole-school aproach to prevention and intervention in early literacy', *Journal of Education for Students Placed at Risk*, Vol. 3, No. 2, pp 133–57

Crystal, D. (1987) *The Cambridge Encyclopaedia of Language*, Cambridge University Press

Cummins, J. (1979) 'Linguistic independence and the educational development of bilingual children', *Review of Educational Research*, Vol.49, pp 222–51

De la Mare, W. (1941) *Bells and Grass*, London: Faber

DES (1991) *Education Observed: The Implementation of the Curricular Requirements of the ERA in 1989–90*, London: HMSO

DfE (1994) *Code of Practice on the Identification and Assessment of Special Educational Needs*, London: HMSO

DfE (1995) *English in the National Curriculum*, London: HMSO

DfEE (1997) Circular 10/97 and DfEE (1998) Circular 4/98, *Teaching: High Status, High Standards*, London: Department for Education and Employment

DfEE (1998) *The National Literacy Strategy Framework for Teaching*, London: Department for Education and Employment

Donaldson, M. (1978) *Children's Minds*, Glasgow: Fontana

Donaldson, M. (1993) *Sense and Sensibility: Some Thoughts on the Teaching of Literacy*, Occasional Paper No. 3, Reading: Reading and Language Information Centre University of Reading. First published 1989, reprinted in Beard, R. (ed.) (1993) op. cit.

Donaldson, M. and Reid, J. (1985) 'Language skills and reading: A developmental perspective', in Clark, M.M. (ed.) (1985) *New Directions in the Study of Reading*, pp 12–25, London and Philadelphia: The Falmer Press

Dowker, A. (1989) 'Rhymes and alliteration in poems elicited from young children', *Journal of Child Language*, 16, pp 181–202

Downing, J. (1979) *Reading and Reasoning*, Edinburgh: W.C. Books

Dyson, A.H. (1989) *Multiple Worlds of Child Writers: Friends Learning to Write*, New York: Teachers College Press

Egoff, S. (1981) *Thursday's Child*, Chicago

Ehri, L.C. (1983) 'Summary of Dorothy C. Ohnmacht's study: The effects of letter knowledge on achievement in reading in the first grade', in Gentile, L.M., Kamil, M.L. and Blanchard, J.S. (eds) *Reading Research Revisited*, pp 141–2, Columbus, OH: Charles E. Morrill

Ehri, L.C.(1992) 'Reconceptualising the development of sight word reading and its relationship to recoding', in Gough, P., Ehri, L.C. and Treiman, R. (eds) (1992) *Reading Acquisition*, Hilsdale, New Jersey: Lawrence Erlbaum Assoc.

Ehri, L.C. (1995) 'Phases of development in learning to read words by sight', *Journal of Research in Reading*, Vol. 18, No. 2, pp 116–26

Ehri, L.C. and Wilce, L.S. (1985) 'Movement into reading: Is the first stage of printed word learning visual or phonetic?' *Reading Research Quarterly*, Vol. 20, pp 163–79

Evans, J. (ed.) (1998) *What's in the Picture? Responding to Illustrations in Picture Books*, London: Paul Chapman Publishing

Ferreiro, E. and Teberosky, A. (1982) *Literacy Before Schooling*, London: Heinemann

Fisher, R.(1992) *Early Literacy and the Teacher*, UKRA

Frith, U. (ed.) (1980a) *Cognitive Processes in Spelling*, New York: Academic Press

Frith, U. (1980b) 'Unexpected spelling problems', in Frith, U. (ed.) (1980a) op. cit., pp 495–516

Frith, U. (1985) 'Beneath the surface of developmental dyslexia', in Patterson, K.E., Coltheart, M. and Marshall, J. (eds) (1985) *Surface Dyslexia*, London: LEA

Frith, U. and Snowling, M. (1983) 'Reading for meaning and reading for sound in autistic and dyslexic children', *British Journal of Developmental Psychology*, 1, pp 329–42

Funnell, E. and Stuart, M. (eds) (1995) *Learning to Read*, Oxford: Blackwell

Gee, J.P.(1992) *The Social Mind: Language, Ideology and Social Practice*, New York: Bergin & Garvey

Gentry, J.R. (1981) 'Learning to spell developmentally', *Reading Teacher*, Vol. 34, No. 4, pp 378–81

Gibson, E.J. and Levin, H. (1975) *The Psychology of Reading*, Cambridge, MA: MIT Press

Goodman, K.S. (1972) 'Reading: The key is in children's language', *The Reading Teacher*, March, pp 505–8

Goodman, K.S. (1973) 'Psycholinguistic universals in the reading process', in Smith, F. (ed.) (1973) *Psycholinguistics and Reading*, New York: Holt Rhinehart & Winston

Goodman, K.S. (1976) 'Reading: A psycholinguistic guessing game', in Singer, H. and Ruddell, R.B. (eds) (1976) *Theoretical Models and Processes of Reading*, pp 497–508, Newark, DE: International Reading Association

Goodman, K.S. and Goodman Y.M. (1979) 'Learning to read is natural', in Resnick, L.B. and Weaver, P.A. (eds) (1979) *Theory and Practice of Early Reading*, Vol. 1, pp 137–54, Hillsdale, NJ: Erlbaum

Goodman, Y.M. (1980) 'The roots of literacy', in Douglass, M.P. (ed.) (1980) *Reading: A Humanising Experience*, Claremont: Claremont Graduate School

Goodman, Y. (1991) 'The development of initial literacy', in Carter, R. (1991) *Knowledge about Language and the Curriculum, The Link Reader*, London: Hodder & Stoughton

Goswami, U. and Bryant, P. (1990) *Phonological Skills and Learning to Read*, Hove: Lawrence Erlbaum & Associates

Goswami, U. (1995) 'Rhyme in children's early reading', in Beard, R. (ed.) (1995) op. cit.

Graham, J. (1998) 'Turning the visual into the verbal: Children reading wordless books', in Evans, J. (ed.) (1998) op. cit.

Gregory, E.(1996) *Making Sense of a New World: Learning to Read in a Second Language*, London: Paul Chapman Publishing

Hall, E.T. (1959) *The Silent Language*, NK: Doubleday

Hall, N. (1987) *The Emergence of Literacy*, Sevenoaks: Hodder & Stoughton

Halliday, M.A.K. (1975) *Learning How to Mean: Explorations in the Development of Language*, London: Arnold

Halliday, M.A.K. (1978) *Language as a Social Semiotic: The Social Interpretation of Language and Meaning*, London: Edward Arnold

Harris, M. (1992) *Language Experience and Early Language Development: From Input to Uptake*, Hove: Lawrence Erlbaum

Hatcher, P.J., Hulme, C. and Ellis, A.W. (1994) 'Helping to overcome reading failure by combining the teaching of reading and phonological skills', in Funnell, E. and Stuart, M. (eds) (1995) op. cit.

Heath, S.B. (1982) 'What no bedtime story means: Narrative skills at home and school', *Language in Society*, 11, pp 49–76

Hester, H. (1983) *Stories in the Multicultural Classroom*, London: Harcourt Brace Jovanovich

Hester, H. (1990) 'Stages of English learning', in *Patterns of Learning: The Primary Language Record and The National Curriculum*, Centre for Language in Primary Education

HMI (1978) *Primary Education in England: A Survey by HM Inspectors of Schools*, London: HMSO

HMI (1991) *The Teaching and Learning of Reading in Primary Schools*, London: Department of Education and Science

HMSO (1967) *Children and Their Primary Schools (The Plowden Report)*, London: HMSO

HMSO (1975) *A Language for Life* (The Bullock Report), Report of the Committee of Inquiry appointed by the Secretary of State for Education and Science, London: HMSO

Hobsbaum, A. (1997) 'Reading Recovery: A lifeline for some', in McClelland (ed.) (1997) op. cit.

Holdaway, D. (1979) *Foundations of Literacy*, Gosford, NSW: Scholastic Publications

Holdaway, D. (1982) 'Shared book experience: Teaching reading using favourite books', *Theory into Practice*, Vol. XXI, No. 4, pp 293–300

House of Commons Education, Science and Arts Committee (1991) *Standards of Reading in Primary Schools*, Third Report of 1990/91 Session, Vol 1, London: HMSO

Hurry, J.(1995) 'What is so special about Reading Recovery?' *The Curriculum Journal*, Vol. 7, No. 1, pp 93–108

Kennedy, M.M., Birman, B.F. and Demaline, R.E. (1986) *The Effectiveness of Chapter 1 Services*, Washington, DC, Office of Educational Research and Improvement, U S Department of Education.

Kintgen, E.R., Kroll, B.M. and Rose, M. (1988) *Perspectives on Literacy*, Carbondale, IL: Southern Illinois University Press

Kress, G.R. (1997) *Before Writing: Rethinking the Paths to Literacy*, London: Routledge

Kress, G. and Van Leeuwen, T. (1996) *Reading Images the Grammar of Graphic Design*, London: Routledge

Liberman, I.Y., Shankweiler, D., Fischer, F.W. and Carter, B. (1974) 'Explicit syllable and phoneme segmentation in young children', *Journal of Experimental Psychology*, 18, 201–12

Littlefair, A.B. (1991) *Reading All Types of Writing*, Milton Keynes: Open University Press

Littlefair, A B. (1993) 'The "good book": Non-narrative aspects', in Beard, R. (ed.) (1993) op. cit.

Lundberg, I., Frost, J. and Peterson, O. (1988) 'Effects of an extensive program for stimulating phonological awareness in pre-school children', *Reading Research Quarterly*, 23, 263–84

Mackay, D., Thomson, B. and Shaub, P. (1970) *Breakthrough to Literacy: Schools Council Programme in Linguistics and English Teaching*, London: Longman

Mallet, M. (1992) *Making Facts Matter: Reading Non-Fiction 5–11*, Paul Chapman Publishing

Marsh, G., Friedman, M., Welch, V. and Desberg, P. (1980) 'The development of strategies in spelling', in Frith, U. (ed.) (1980a) op. cit.

McClelland, N. (ed.) (1997) *Building a Literate Nation: The Strategic Agenda for Literacy Over the Next Five Years*, Stoke-on-Trent: Trentham Books

McGaw, B., Long, M.G., Morgan, G. and Rosier, M.J. (1989) *Literacy and Numeracy in Australian Schools*, ACER Research Monograph No. 34, Hawthorn, Victoria: ACER

McGee, L., Lomax, R. and Head, M. (1984) *Young Children's Functional Reading*, Paper presented at the National Reading Conference, Florida

McGee, L., Lomax, R. and Head, M. (1988) 'Young children's written language knowledge: What environmental and functional print reading reveals', *Journal of Reading Behaviour*, 20, pp 99–118

McKenzie, M. and Warlow, A. (1977) *Reading Matters*, London: Hodder & Stoughton

Meek, M. (1981) 'Handing down the magic', in Salmon, P. (ed.) (1981) *Coming to Know*, London: Routledge, Kegan & Paul

Meek, M. (1982) *Learning To Read*, London: Bodley Head

Meek, M. (1988) *How Texts Teach What Readers Learn*, Thimble Press

Meek, M. (1991) *On Being Literate*, London: Bodley Head

Moll, L.C. (ed.) (1990) *Vygotsky and Education*, Cambridge: Cambridge University Press

Morais, J., Bertleson, P., Cary, L. and Alegria, J. (1986) 'Literacy training and speech segmentation', *Cognition*, 24, pp 45–64

Morais, J., Cary, L., Alegria, J. and Bertelson, P. (1979) 'Does awareness of speech as a sequence of phonemes arise spontaneously', *Cognition*, 7, 323–31

Mortimore, P., Sammons, P., Stoll, L., Lewis, D.R. and Ecob, R. (1988) *School Matters*, London: Open Books

Neale, M.D. (1989) *The Neale Analysis of Reading Ability*, revised edition, Windsor: NFER

Nelson, K.(1973) 'Structure and strategy in learning to talk', *Monographs of the Society for Research in Child Development*, 38 (1–2, serial no. 149)

Ninio, A. (1980) 'Picture-book reading in mother–infant dyads belonging to two subgroups in Israel', *Child Development*, 51, pp 587–90

Ninio, A. and Bruner, J. (1978) 'The achievement and antecedents of labelling', *Journal of Child Language*, 5, pp 1–15

Ofsted (1996) *The Teaching of Reading in 45 Inner London Primary Schools*, London: HMSO

Parkes, B. (1998) 'Nursery children using illustrations in shared readings and re-readings', in Evans, J. (ed.) (1998) op. cit.

Pedersen, E., Faucher, T.A. and Eaton, W.W. (1978) 'A new perspective on the effects of first-grade teachers on children's subsequent adult status', *Harvard Educational Review*, Vol. 48, No. 1, pp 1–31

Perrera, K. (1993) 'The "good book": Linguistic aspects', in Beard, R. (ed.) (1993) op. cit.

Piluski, J.J. (1994) 'Preventing reading failure: A review of five effective programmes', *The Reading Teacher*, 48, pp 31–9

Pumfrey, P.D. and Elliott, C.D. (1992) 'A reaction', *British Psychological Society*, Education Section Review, Vol. 16, No. 1, pp 15–19

Purcell-Gates, V. (1996) 'Stories, coupons and the TV guide: Relationship between home literacy experiences and emergent literacy knowledge', *Reading Research Quarterly*, Vol. 31, No. 4, pp 406–28

Rayner, K. and Pollatsek, A. (1987) 'Eye movements in reading: A tutorial review', in Coltheart, M. (ed.) (1987) *Attention and Performance XII: The Psychology of Reading*, pp 327–53, London: Erlbaum Assoc.

Read, C., Zhang, Y., Nie, H. and Ding, B. (1986) 'The ability to manipulate speech sounds depends on knowing alphabetic spelling', *Cognition*, 24, pp 31–4.

Reason, R. and Boote, R. (1994) *Helping Children with Reading and Spelling: A Special Needs Manual*, London and New York: Routledge

Reading Recovery National Network (1998) *Book Bands*, Kent: Orchard Publishing

Reid, J.F. (1993) 'Reading and spoken language: The nature of the links', in Beard, R. (ed.) (1993) op. cit.

Riley, J.L. (1994) *The Development of Literacy in the First Year of School*, Unpublished Ph.D. thesis, University of London

Riley, J.L. (1995a) 'The transition phase between emergent literacy and conventional beginning reading: New research findings', *Journal for Tutors for Advanced Courses for Teachers of Young Children*, Vol. 16, No. 1

Riley, J.L. (1995b) 'The relationship between adjustment to school and success in reading by the end of the reception year', *Early Child Development and Care*, Vol. 114, pp 25–38

Riley, J.L. (1996) *The Teaching of Reading: The Development of Literacy in the Early Years of School*, London: Paul Chapman Publishing

Rosen, H. (1985) *Stories and Meanings*, Sheffield: National Association for the Teaching of English (49 Broomgrove Road, Sheffield S10 2NA)

Rosenblatt, L. (1938) *Literature as Exploration*, New York: Appleton-Century

Sammons, P. (1994) 'Gender, ethnic and socio-economic difference in attainment and progress: A longitudinal analysis of student achievement over nine years', *British Educational Research Journal*, Vol. 21, No. 4

Sammons, P., Nuttall, D., Cuttance, P. and Thomas, S. (1994) 'Continuity of school effects: A longitudinal analysis of primary and secondary school effects on GCSE performance', Submitted to *School Effectiveness and School Improvement Journal*

Sassoon, R. (1995) *The Acquisition of a Second Writing System*, Oxford: Intellect

SCAA (1995) *Boys and English*, Schools Council and Curriculum Authority

Schools Examination and Assessment Council (SEAC) (1991) 'Assessment of Performance Unit Report on the 1988 APU Survey', pp 127–37 in *Assessment Matters No. 4: Language and Learning*, London: HMSO

Senechal, M., Lefevre, J., Thomas, E. and Daley, K.E. (1998) 'Differential effects of home literacy experiences on the development of oral and written language', *Reading Research Quarterly*, Vol. 33, No. 1, pp 96–116

Short, K. (1986) *Literacy as a Collaborative Experience*, Unpublished doctoral dissertation, Indiana University

Siraj-Blatchford, I. (1995) *The Early Years: Laying the Foundation of Racial Equality*, Stoke-on-Trent: Trentham Books

Skuttnab-Kangas, T. (1984) 'Multilingualism and the education of minority children', in Skutnab-Kangas, T. and Cummins, J. (eds) *Minority Education*, Clevedon: Multilingual Matters

Slavin, R.E., Madden, N.A., Dolan, N.J., Wasik, B.J., Ross, S.M., Smith, L.J. and Dianda, M. (1996) 'Success for all: A summary of research', *Journal for Education for Students Placed at Risk*, 1, pp 41–76

Stanovich, K.E. (1986) 'Matthew effects in reading: Some consequences of individual differences in the acquisition of literacy', *Reading Research Quarterly*, 21, pp 360–406

Stanovich, K.E, Cunningham, A.E. and Cramer, B.Q. (1984a) 'Assessing phonological awareness in kindergarten children:issues of task comparabiity', *Journal of Experimental Child Psychology*, 38, pp 175–90

Stanovich, K.E., Cunningham, A.E. and Freeman, D.J. (1984b) 'Intelligence, cognitive skills and early reading progress', *Reading Research Quarterly*, 19, pp 278–303

Stuart, M. (1995) 'Recognising printed words unlocks the door to reading: How do children find the key?' in Funnell, E. and Stuart, M. (eds) (1995) op. cit.

Sulzby, E. (1989) 'Assessment of writing and of children's language while writing', in Morrow, L. and Smith, J. (eds) (1989) *The Role of Assessment in Early Literacy Instruction*, pp 83–109, Englewood Cliffs, NJ: Prentice-Hall

Sulzby, E. (1992) 'Research directions: Transitions from emergent to conventional writing', *Language Arts*, 69 pp 291–7

Sulzby, E. and Teale, W. (1991) 'Emergent literacy', in Barr, J., Kamil, M., Mosenthal, P. and Pearson, D. (eds) (1991) *The Handbook of Reading Research*, Vol. 2, Chapter 26, pp 727–57, London: Longman

Styles, M. and Watson, V. (eds) (1996) *Talking Pictures*, London: Hodder & Stoughton

Taylor, D. and Dorsey-Gaines, C. (1988) *Growing Up Literate*, Portsmouth, NH: Heinemann

Teale, W. (1986) 'Home background and young children's literacy development', in Teale, W.H. and Sulzby, E. (eds) (1986) *Emergent Literacy: Writing and Reading*, Norwood, NJ: Ablex

Tizard, B. (1993) 'Early influences on literacy', in Beard, R. (ed.) (1993) op. cit.

Tizard, B., Blatchford, P., Burke, J., Farquhar, C. and Plewis, I. (1988) *Young Children at School in the Inner City*, Hove and London: Lawrence Erlbaum

Tizard, B. and Hughes, M. (1984) *Young Children Learning*, London: Fontana

Treiman, R. and Baron, J. (1981) 'Segmental analysis: Development and relation to reading ability', in Mackinnon, G.C. and Waller, T.C. (eds) *Reading Research: Advances in Theory and Practice*, Vol. 111, New York: Academic Press

Trevarthen, C. (1993) 'Playing into reality: Conversations with the infant communicator', *Winnicot Studies*, Spring, 7, pp 67–84

Tucker, N. (1981) *The Child and the Book*, Cambridge: Cambridge University Press

Tucker, N. (1993) 'The "good book": The literary and developmental aspects', in Beard, R. (ed.) (1993) op. cit.

Tunmer, W.E., Herriman, M.L. and Nesdale, A.R. (1988) 'Metalinguistic abilities and beginning reading', *Reading Research Quarterly*, 32, pp 134–58

Turner, M. (1990) *Sponsored Reading Failure*, Warlingham, Surrey: IPSET

Turner, M. (1991) 'Finding out', *Support for Learning*, Vol. 6, No. 3, pp 99–102

Turner, M. (1992) 'Organised inferiority? Reading and the National Curriculum', *British Psychological Society Educational Section Review*, Vol. 16, No. 1, pp 1–25

Vygotsky, L.S. (1978) *Mind in Society: The Development of Higher Psychological Processes*, Cambridge, Mass: Harvard University Press

Vygotsky, L.S. (1986) *Thought and Language*, 3rd edition, Cambridge, Mass: MIT Press

Wells, C.G. (1983) 'Talking with children: The complementary roles of parents and teachers', in Donaldson, M., Grieve, R. and Pratt, C. (eds) *Early Childhood Development and Education*, Oxford: Blackwell

Wells, C.G. (1987) *The Meaning Makers: Children Learning Language and Using Language to Learn*, London: Hodder & Stoughton

Wells, C.G. (1988) 'The roots of literacy', *Psychology Today*, 22, pp 20–2

Wells, C.G. and Raban, B. (1978) *Children Learning to Read*, Unpublished Final SSRC Report (lodged in School of Education Library, University of Bristol, 19 Berkeley Square, Bristol)

Whitehead, M. (1997) *The Development of Language and Literacy*, London: Hodder & Stoughton

Wilkinson, A. (1982) *Language and Education*, Oxford University Press

Wray, D. and Lewis, M.(1997) *Extending Literacy: Children Reading and Writing Non-fiction*, London and New York: Routledge

References II

LITERARY REFERENCES

Ahlberg, A. and Ahlberg, J. (1986) *The Jolly Postman or Other People's Letters*, London: Heinemann

Ahlberg, A. and Ahlberg, J. (1991) *The Jolly Christmas Postman*, London: Heinemann

Ahlberg, A. and Ahlberg, J. (1995) *The Jolly Pocket Postman*, London: Heinemann

Briggs, R. (1978) *The Snowman*, London: Hamish Hamilton

Burningham, J. (1977) *Come Away From The Water, Shirley*, London: Cape

Cole, B. (1986) *Princess Smartypants*, London: Picture Lion

Cole, B. (1987) *Prince Cinders*, Hayes: Magi

Fanthorpe, U.E. (1992) *Heck-Verse, Half-Past Two*, Calstock Poets

Felts, S. (1996) *Trees*, London: Tango Books

Holden, E. (1977) *The Country Diary of an Edwardian Lady*, London: Sphere Books Ltd

Holm, A.(1965) *I am David*, Great Britain: Methuen & Co. Ltd

James, S. (1992) *My Friend Whale*, London: Walker

Letterland (1993) *Picture Dictionary*, Letterland Ltd, Barton, Cambridge CB3 7AY

Lloyd, S. (1993) *Jolly Phonics*, Jolly Learning Ltd

Lloyd, S., Wernham, S. and Jolly, C. (1993) *Jolly Learning*, Singapore: Jolly Learning Ltd

McKee, D.(1978) *Tusk Tusk*, London: Anderson Press

McKee, D.(1980) *Not Now Bernard*, London: Anderson Press

Munsch, R.N. (1980) *The Paper Bag Princess*, London: Scholastic

Sauvain, P. (1995) *The Tudors and Stuarts*, Dorchester: Wayland

Appendix

CONDUCTING A RUNNING READING RECORD

The following advice on how to conduct a running reading record is quoted from Marie M. Clay, An Observation Survey of Early Literacy Achievement (1993), pp. 24, 27, 28 and 29. An example of a completed running reading record, using the format suggested by Clay (1993, p. 25), can be found on pages 98 and 99 of this book (Figures 5.3a and 5.3b).

LEARNING TO MAKE A RUNNING RECORD

Learning to take a running record can unsettle teachers. Those who are used to standardised tests and norms question the simplicity of the behaviour records, and so do people who do not like standardised testing.

There is not a lot to learn before you begin taking a running record, just a few conventions. There is no reason to study a new set of concepts or understand something new about the reading process. The first step is a matter of action. You set yourself the task of recording everything that a child says and does as he tries to read the book you have chosen. Once you begin such recording, and after about two hours of initial practice, no matter how much you might be missing, you have made a good start. The more you take the records the more you will notice about children's behaviour. It is not a case of knowing everything first and then applying it. Try yourself out and you will begin to notice a few things that you have not noticed before. Practise some more and you will notice more. As your ear becomes tuned-in to reading behaviours and you gain control over the recording conventions your records will become more and more reliable.

I had been teaching reading and remedial reading for many years when I began my research on emergent reading behaviour. I am still humble about the fact that I had never noticed self-correction behaviour until I started recording everything that children were doing. It was then I found that I had been missing something that was very important.

What we are observing and recording is not something that is peculiar to the child who is learning to read. If I take some adult volunteers and ask them to read some ordinary everyday reading materials their reading behaviour can be broken down so that we can observe the same kinds of behaviour that occur in children's reading. A smudgy carbon copy, a poor fax copy, a Churchill speech in i.t.a., a newspaper extract with misprints where the lines have been misplaced, or a very difficult scientific or medical text will break down the reading behaviours of competent adults and one can observe self-correction, word-by-word reading and even the use of a pointing finger to locate themselves on the text. Everybody's reading behaviour can be broken down under difficulties.

Make a record of each child reading his three little books or book selections. Use ticks for each correct response and record every error in full. A sample reading of 100 to 200 words from each text is required. This should take about 10 minutes. At the early reading level when the child is reading the very simplest texts the number of words may fall below 100 but if three texts are attempted (selected from caption books or first readers or teacher-made books or child-dictated text) this will be satisfactory even though the extracts themselves are short. . . .

SOME CONVENTIONS USED FOR RECORDING

1 Mark every word read correctly with a tick (or check). A record of the first five pages of the 'Ready to Read' (1963) book *Early in the Morning* that was 100 percent correct would look like this. (The lines indicate page breaks.)

Bill is asleep.	✓	✓	✓
'Wake up, Bill,'	✓	✓	✓
said Peter.	✓	✓	
Sally is asleep.	✓	✓	✓
'Wake up, Sally,'	✓	✓	✓
said Mother.	✓	✓	
Father is shaving.	✓	✓	✓

2 Record a wrong response with the text under it.

Child: home

Text: house   [One error]

3 If a child tries several times to read a word, record all his trials.

Child: here	*h—*	*home*	
Text: house			[One error]

Child: h—	*ho—*	*home*	
Text: home			[No error]

4 If a child succeeds in correcting a previous error this is recorded as 'self-correction' (written SC). Note that example 3 did not result in a self-correction.

Child: where	*when*	SC	
Text: were			[No error]

5 If no response is given to a word it is recorded with a dash. Insertion of a word is recorded over a dash.

No response Insertion

Child: —	*Child: here*	[In each case
Text: house	Text: —	one error]

6 If the child baulks, unable to proceed because he is aware he has made an error and cannot correct it, or because he cannot attempt the next word, he is told the word (written T).

Child: home		
Text: house	T	[One error]

7 An appeal for help (A) from the child is turned back to the child for further effort before using T as in 6 above. Say 'You try it'.

Child: —	*A*	*here*	
Text: house	—	T	[One error]

8 Sometimes the child gets into a state of confusion and it is necessary to extricate him. The most detached method of doing this is to say 'Try that again', marking TTA on the record. This would not involve any teaching, but the teacher may indicate where the child should begin again.

It is a good idea to put square brackets around the first set of muddled behaviour, enter the TTA, remember to count that as one error only, and then begin a fresh record of the problem text. An example of this record would be:

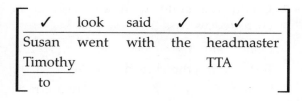

[One error]

9 Repetition (R) is not counted as error behaviour. Sometimes it is used to confirm a previous attempt. Often results in self-correction. It is useful to record it as it often indicates how much sorting out the child is doing. 'R', standing for repetition, is used to indicate repetition of a word, with R_2 or R_3 indicating the number of repetitions. If the child goes back over a group of words, or returns to the beginning of the line or sentence in his repetition, the point to which he returns is shown by an arrow.

Child:	*Here is the home*	R	SC	
Text:	Here is the house			[No error]

10 Sometimes the child re-reads the text (repetition) and corrects some but not all errors. The following example shows the recording of this behaviour.

Child:	*a*	SC	*house*	R	[One error]
Text:	the		home		[One SC]

11 Directional attack on the printed text is recorded by telling the child to 'Read it with your finger'.

Left to right	L $\longrightarrow$ R
Right to left	L $\longleftarrow$ R
Snaking	
Bottom to top	B $\longrightarrow$ T

For special purposes teachers or researchers may wish to develop their own conventions for scoring other behaviours which they notice. Some behaviours may be specific to, or important for, a particular teaching programme. For example, pausing can be recorded by a slash, /. Some researchers who have been concerned with the length of pausing have used a convention borrowed from linguistics which allows for pauses of four different lengths. These are quickly recorded as

$$/ \qquad // \qquad /\!\!/\!\!\!- \qquad \#$$

I would caution against attention to pausing unless there is a special reason for wishing to record it. *In research studies it has not yet yielded clear messages about the reading process* (Clay and Imlach, 1971). It adds little to the teacher's interpretation of her record and may cause confusion. Pausing behaviour is sensitive to the instructional programme and may have been induced by the ways in which children are being taught. Pauses do not necessarily mean that 'reading work' (as I discuss this concept in Clay, 1991), is taking place. *It would be important not to read things into a record of pausing interpretations for which there was no other evidence.*

A running record from a child who is making many errors is harder to take and score but the rule is to record all behaviour, and analyse objectively what is recorded.

Reliability

Taped recordings of such reading observations taken from four children over the period of one year were available and were used to check on the reliability of such records (0.98 for error scoring and 0.68 for self-correction scoring, Clay, 1966).

A number of trends became obvious during these reliability tests.

- For beginning readers, observers can take running records which give reliable accuracy scores with a small amount of training.
- The effect of poor observation is to reduce the number of errors recorded and increase the accuracy rate. As the observer's skill in recording at speed increases, so the error scores tend to rise.
- To record all error behaviour in full, as against only tallying its occurrence, takes much more practice (but provides more evidence of the child's strategies).
- Observations for poor readers require longer training to reach agreement on scoring standards because of the complex error behaviour.
- Information is lost in the taped observation, especially motor behaviour and visual survey, but observation of vocal behaviour tends to be improved.
- Reliability probably drops as reading accuracy level falls because there is more error behaviour to be recorded in the same time span.

For research work the most reliable records would be obtained by scoring an observation immediately following its manual recording, and rechecking immediately with a taped observation.

ANALYSING THE READING RECORD

From the running record of reading behaviour containing al the child's behaviour on his current book, consider what is happening as the child reads.

Some conventions for scoring the records

In counting the number of errors, some arbitrary decisions must be made but the following have been found workable.

1 Credit the child with any correct or corrected words.

Child:	to	the	shops	
Text:	for	the	bread	
Score:	✗	✓	✗	[Two errors]

2 There is no penalty for trials which are eventually correct.

A
Child:	want	won't	went	SC	
Text:	went				[No error]
Score:	—	—	✓		[One SC]

B
Child:	where	we	when	were	SC	
Text:	were					[No error]
Score:	—	—	—	✓		[One SC]

3 Insertions add errors so that a child can have more errors than there are words in a line.

Child:	The	train	went	toot,	toot,	toot
Text:	The	little	engine	sighed		
Score:	✓	✗	✗	✗	✗	✗

[Five errors]

4 However, the child cannot receive a minus score for a page. The lowest page score is 0.

5 *Omissions.* If a line or sentence is omitted each word is counted as an error.

   If pages are omitted (perhaps because two pages were turned together) they are not counted as errors. Note that in this case, the number of words on the omitted pages must be deducted from the Running Words Total before calculation.

6 *Repeated errors.* If the child makes an error (e.g., 'run' for 'ran') and then substitutes this word repeatedly, it counts as an error every time; but substitution of a proper name (e.g., 'Mary' for 'Molly') is counted only the first time.

7 *Multiple errors and self-correction.* If a child makes two or more errors (e.g., reads a phrase wrongly) each word is an error. if he then corrects all these errors each corrected word is a self-correction.

8 *Broken words.* Where a word is pronounced as two words (e.g., a/way) even when this is backed up by pointing as if it were two words, this is regarded as an error of pronunciation, not as a reading error unless what is said is matched to a different word. Such things a 'pitcher' for 'picture' and 'gonna' for 'going to' are counted as correct.

9 *Inventions* defeat the system. When the young child is creatively producing his own version of the story the scoring system finally breaks down and the judgement 'inventing' is recorded for that page, story or book.

10 *'Try that again'.* When the child is in a tangle this instruction, which does not involve teaching, can be given. It counts as one error and only the second attempt is scored.

11 *Fewest errors.* If there are alternate ways of scoring responses a general principle is to choose the method that give the *fewest* possible errors as in B below.

A *Child:* We went for the bread
Text: You went to the shop for the bread
Score: ✗   ✓   ✗   ✓   ✗   ✗   ✗
[Six errors]

B *Child:* We went   for the bread
Text: You went to the shop for the bread
Score: ✗   ✓   ✗   ✗   ✗   ✓   ✓   ✓
[Four errors]

Index

Page references in italics indicate figures

National Writing Project viii
near rhymes 49
non-fiction 154
    criteria for choice of 162
    evidence of problems with use 155–6
    helping pupils 156, 160–2
    rationale for use of 154–5
    reading to children 39
    types
        expositionary texts 157–9
        narrative 156–7
        non-narrative 157
Not Now Bernard (McKee) 146

observation
    of child reading 93–4
        choice of text 97
        NC (Pre Level 1) 60–1, 117
        NC Level 1 (Early Stage) 62–3, 118–19
        NC Level 1 (Later Stage) 64, 120
        NC Level 2 65
    of reception child 80–1
    of writing 102
    see also assessment; running reading records
onsets 49, 50, 88
open questions 14
oracy 1
    inter-related with literacy 17, 23
    see also speech
orthographic awareness 50–1, 94
    developing 51, 87, 88, 88–9, 92
    development studies 55–9
    Frith's phase theory 51–5, 91
    records of assessment of 80–1
    teaching approaches
        NC (Pre-Level 1) 62, 118
        NC Level 1 (Early Stage) 63–4, 120
        NC Level 1 (Later Stage) 65, 121
        NC Level 2 66
orthographic phase of print-processing 53–5, 91, 101

Paper Bag Princess, The (Munsch) 149
parents
    attitudes and child's literacy difficulties 110–11
    and direct teaching of children 74
    education level and child's literacy 72
    involvement in education of bilingual children 130
    and pre-school language development 8–11
    see also adults; mothers
perception 50
    see also print awareness
personality and literacy difficulties 110

phonemes 46, 46–7, 48, 49, 88
    grapheme-phoneme correspondence 47, 48, 53, 87, 101
    onsets 49
phonemic segmentation 46, 54, 87, 88
    difficulties in 46–7, 48
phonetic spelling 101
phonological awareness 46, 49, 95
    developing *86*, 87–8
    importance of sound processing skills 46
    and learning to read 47–8
        alphabetic code 48–9
        rhyme and rime 49, 49–50
    records of assessment of 81
    teaching approaches
        NC (Pre-Level 1) 61–2, 117–18
        NC Level 1 (Early Stage) 63, 119
        NC Level 1 (Later Stage) 64, 121
        NC Level 2 66
physical impairment and literacy difficulties 110
picture books 70, 147–8
    longer texts 150
    as polysemic texts 148–50
    use as a way into print 150–1
    ways support early reading 151
    wordless 150
picture cues 29, 35
play
    and additional language learning 133, 133–5
    and language practice 17–18
polysemic texts, picture books as 148–50
pre-reading 69
pre-school children
    awareness of roots of literacy 69–70
    home literacy experiences 71–5
    importance of capitalising on pre-school knowledge 76–8
    knowledge of literacy 70–1, 85
    language development 2–5, 7–11
prediction 21, 31, 31–2, *33*, 34, 35, 36, 87
    confirming 37–8
primary education
    importance in improving standards of literacy vi–vii
    and National Literacy Strategy ix
Prince Cinders (Cole) 149
Princess Smarty Pants (Cole) 149
print awareness 36, 50–1, 94
    developing 51, 87, 88, 88–9, 92
    Frith's phase theory 51–5, 90–1
    records of assessment of 80–1
    teaching approaches
        NC (Pre-Level 1) 62, 118
        NC Level 1 (Early Stage) 63–4, 120